Ca   ess

ALLWORTH PRESS, NEW YORK

4-95   # 31603229

Published by Allworth Press, an imprint of
Allworth Communications, Inc.
10 East 23rd Street, New York, NY 10010

Distributor to the trade in the United States and Canada:
Consotrium Book Sales & Distribution, Inc.
1045 Westgate Drive, Saint Paul, MN 55114-0165

Book design by Douglas Design Associates, New York, NY

Typography by Sharp Designs, Holt, MI

ISBN: 1-880559-16-1

Library of Congress Catalog Card Number: 94-70296

CONTENTS

Preface   *7*

Introduction   *11*

PART I • YOUR CAREER

Chapter 1 • Career Self-Reliance and Fulfillment   *17*
• Attaining Success and Fulfillment   *17*
• Developing a Career Plan   *19*
• Our Career Life-Cycles   *20*

Chapter 2 • The New Job Market   *25*
• The Future Job Outlook   *26*
• Occupational Profiles for 1990–2005   *28*
• Tomorrow's Job Earnings   *45*
• The Right Job Skills   *48*

Chapter 3 • Finding and Keeping the Right Job   *51*
• Marketing Your Talents   *51*
• Finding Career and Job Information   *52*
• Creating an Effective Resumé   *55*
• Being Successful at Job Interviews   *59*
• Being a Participant   *61*
• Keeping a Good Image   *63*

Chapter 4 • Dealing With Job Transitions   *67*
- Life as a Business Cycle   *67*
- Becoming Oriented to a New Job   *69*
- Handling Job Moves   *70*
- Preparing for Unemployment   *73*

Chapter 5 • Pursuing Your Own Business   *77*
- Going into Business for Yourself   *77*
- Your Next Steps   *80*
- Where Are Your Customers?   *82*
- Should You Buy an Existing Business?   *84*
- Buying a Franchise   *86*
- Choosing Your Form of Business Organization   *89*
- Recordkeeping   *93*
- Working with Professionals   *95*
- Laws That May Apply to Your Business   *97*
- Learning from Experience and Networking   *98*

PART II • DEVELOPING CAREER SKILLS
Chapter 6 • Becoming Proficient With Computers   *105*
- Making Use of Computers   *105*
- The Value of Information   *108*
- Understanding Computer Software   *110*
- Steps to Using Computer Software   *112*
- Acquiring Computer Skills and Equipment   *114*

Chapter 7 • Communicating Effectively   *117*
- Writing for Success   *117*
- Effective Speaking and Presentation   *120*

Chapter 8 • Negotiating Successfully   *125*
- Approaches to Negotiation   *125*
- The Elements of Successful Negotiation   *126*
- Planning for a Successful Negotiation   *129*

- The Negotiation Process 132
- Handling Conflict in Negotiations 134

PART III · YOUR MONEY AND RESOURCES
Chapter 9 · Money Management 139
- Financial Planning for the Nineties and Beyond 139
- Setting Financial Goals 140
- Cash Flow Management 147
- Selecting a Financial Institution 150
- Investment Planning 152
- Effective Estate Planning 155
- Estate Planning Devices 156
- Setting Up Your Estate Plan 158

Chapter 10 · Maintaining Good Insurance 161
- Do You Need Insurance? 161
- Reviewing Your Life Insurance Needs 162
- What Type of Life Insurance? 164
- Using Life Insurance to Meet Financial Goals 167
- Keeping Good Health Insurance 170
- HMOs as a Health Care Alternative 172
- Lowering Your Auto Insurance Costs 173

Chapter 11 · Achieving Good Credit 177
- Building a Credit History 177
- Conducting Your Own Credit Review 178
- Correcting Errors in Your Credit Report 181
- Dealing with a Poor Credit History 182
- Coping with Mounting Bills 183
- Understanding the Cost of Credit 184

Chapter 12 · Protecting Your Privacy 185
- Protecting Credit Records 185
- Keeping Your Medical and InsuranceRecords Confidential 188

- Avoiding Mail and Telemarketing Frauds   *189*
- Safeguarding Your Privacy with Telecommunications   *191*
- Protecting Yourself From Telephone Fraud   *192*

Conclusion   *197*

Appendix   *199*
- Sources of State and Local Job Information   *199*
- Selected Bibliography   *209*
- Sample Functional Resumé   *213*
- Sample Chronological Resumé   *214*

Index   *215*

PREFACE

Smart Maneuvers provides a comprehensive vision of how to live and work successfully in a time of great change. Whether you are a recent college graduate or in mid-career, the factors that made for success in the past may no longer serve you. The work place has changed dramatically. With these changes have come new stresses on career, family life, and health; stresses that often seem beyond the ability of any individual to control. From the ubiquitous computer with its high-technology benefits, to international competition, to changing demographics, to rising concerns over health and wellness, the world of tomorrow promises to be far different than we might imagine. The lessons of the past may not serve you well in the information age, nor can you hope to attain success and fulfillment with a fragmented vision of how to handle career and quality-of-life issues.

Vast changes have and will continue to be introduced into the workplace, including downsizing, diversification, project teams, job retraining, flex-time, job sharing, telecommuting, and many, many more. Although some of these changes will be difficult to manage, they can also offer new challenges and opportunities if you prepare yourself to take advantage of them. New work and career options can allow greater control, and a chance to improve the quality of your life by a more even blend of work, family, and leisure. *Smart Maneuvers* will help you utilize the various options to redesign your life for success and fulfillment.

The information age will continue to challenge every facet of your life. You will change the way you view work and career. The linear life plan is quickly coming to an end. It is being replaced by a more variable one, offering new opportunities and choices at every stage in life. For example, you may retire several times or never retire at all. You are likely to go back to school and learn new skills. You will probably change your career four or five times during your life.

Smart Maneuvers will help the worker of the future understand the importance of being flexible and staying independent. The days of loyal life-time employment are gone. Even when on payroll, you must see yourself, not merely as an employee, but as a provider of skills that have intrinsic value. It will become crucial for you to understand tomorrow's job market and develop the skills necessary for career success and self-reliance. You will need to focus on making good career choices, continuing your professional growth and development, handling job changes, and overcoming layoffs or unemployment. You must be effective with your resumé, interviewing, and networking to achieve maximum advantage. You must be willing to explore alternative career prospects—including starting your own business.

Although career success can oftentimes translate into financial security, you should always practice good money management, budgeting, wise investing, and maintaining the best insurance coverage. You should also maintain a good credit record and verify your credit report periodically, because most of the big ticket items in your life will depend on your access to credit. It will be important to keep your financial, tax, and vital records well-organized and in a secure place.

To be fulfilled will require career, financial, and personal success. Moreover, career success, financial prosperity, wellness, and quality of life issues have become more and more interrelated. *Smart Maneuvers* hopes to help you find success by taking an active role in your own personal development, by being a participant at work and in the community, and by developing the skills to become proficient with computers, communicate effectively, and negotiate successfully. These points of personal and professional enhancement will be vital to successful life and work in the nineties and beyond.

SMART MANEUVERS

INTRODUCTION

*O*ur world has shifted from an industrial society to an informational one. This new age of high-tech and super information will require that we constantly focus on career, personal development, credit, finances, privacy, and other factors which will make for success and fulfillment. Factors such as career planning, understanding tomorrow's job market, acquiring the right skills, and managing our talents and resources will determine whether we succeed or fail. It is imperative that we are proactive in managing all of these issues if we are to take control of our career and personal success.

The future business climate will provide less job security, reduced autonomy and demand greater performance from everyone. Business organizations will be flatter as layers of middle management disappear and many companies go through a "decruiting" phase. Career advancement will no longer be primarily a function of longevity, endurance, and loyalty. Rather, performance, flexibility, creativity, and entrepreneurship are likely to be the real measures of future success. Professional growth and achievement will most likely come from the ability to effectively use data and other information to make decisions and to identify new business opportunities.

Modifications will be made to our physical work environment with technology and computerization dominating every aspect. Lower-level employees will be used more and more to process and analyze information and for routine decision-making. They will be aided by breakthroughs in both computer hardware and software, including interactive work stations, enhanced graphics, and worldwide computer networks. We will be able to transfer memos, graphs, scientific data, and legal documents; see co-workers in distant locations; and attend meetings without leaving our desks. Thus, it will be a necessity that we become computer literate and maintain some reason-able proficiency in using computers to remain competitive in this high-tech world.

Access to information about our firms and their business, problems, successes, objectives, competitive strategies, and financial performance will be crucial to our career success. Again, the computer will be a powerful tool in getting and managing information. Reading the company's financial reports, internal publications on business activities and new products, and relevant trade and business periodicals aids in professional advancement. Learning how to find and access needed information has become a prerequisite to success.

Surviving in tomorrow's workplace means making sure that our skills and functions add real value to a business by directly or indirectly generating revenues or profits. This requires avoiding jobs and career paths that involve routine or pre-defined decision-making, or ones that are purely advisory. These are the areas most likely to be adversely affected by business downsizing.

To be successful we must have a macro, long-range vision focusing on where we ultimately want to be. Although our career goals will change over our lifetime, we should review every potential opportunity, position, and employer in terms of our long-range career objectives. Sometimes we may have to accept short-term trade-offs for some long-term benefits. Important training opportunities and contacts can be gained from some low-paying and otherwise unexceptional jobs.

We should always try to broaden our background and skills, while at the same time specializing in at least one area;

preferably two or more. Care should be taken not to limit ourselves to isolated and overly specialized job assignments; rather we should keep our awareness for broader responsibilities that may become available to us while in our current position.

Look at college or other professional training for further development; particularly if employers will pay for the costs. Most major corporations and professional associations offer educational assistance and continuing education as part of their benefits packages.

We need to take full advantage of corporate-sponsored training—which is the fastest-growing type of education in America. Over fifty billion dollars are spent by corporate America each year on training. Employees are not only trained for new positions and careers, but how to deal with family and personal issues.

Flex-time and telecommuting will also offer many options for redefining conventional work arrangements. The ability to set our own work hours and work out of our home or in the car will offer a sense of independence and self-determination.

The decline in the amount of time spent working is a major change of our industrialized and computerized society. Today, the average American spends only about fourteen percent of his or her life working compared with about thirty to forty percent for early agrarian cultures. This leisure time will provide the freedom to explore a myriad of recreational, developmental, and professional choices.

Long-range career planning is critical in defining objectives, accomplishing goals, and attaining career success and fulfillment. This requires periodically assessing our skills and how they match up with our career goals. Career information, career counseling, and networking are essential in this process.

Organizations are in constant need of people with valuable skills and talents. Everyone needs to market their talents by creating an effective resumé and being successful on job interviews. These should be seen as opportunities to highlight background, experience, and other qualifications.

Dealing with transition will be a part of everyone's life as people move in, up, down, or out of organizations. Being flexible, preparing for, and recognizing change are the key to managing transition on and off the job.

As corporate America goes through downsizing, starting a business has become an attractive career alternative. Entrepreneurship can enhance a person's background and experience, offer new career paths, and provide additional income. However, it first requires an assessment of entrepreneurial skills, an analysis of business opportunities, the availability of adequate resources, and effective networking.

Whether we are in business for ourselves or working as corporate employees, we must continue with our professional development and self-improvement. Acquiring computer proficiency, effective communication and negotiation skills are ways to improve job performance and remain competitive.

Effective financial planning and money management contributes to personal success and fulfillment. This involves setting financial goals, budgeting, investment and estate planning, and selecting a good financial institution. Maintaining good credit and insurance are important corollaries to effective money management and financial stability.

Protection of privacy and safeguarding against consumer frauds are also important issues for everyone in this information society. Adequate steps must be taken to ensure that credit, medical and insurance records are kept confidential. Recognizing and avoiding the problems of credit card, mail, and telemarketing fraud will help in becoming a smart consumer.

Managing our talents and resources and adapting to change are the key elements to success and fulfillment in the dynamic world of high tech and super information.

PART ONE

YOUR CAREER

CHAPTER ONE

CAREER SELF-RELIANCE AND FULFILLMENT

*U*nderstanding tomorrow's job market and effective career management are essential to finding success in the nineties and beyond. Everyone must define career goals and develop a career plan in order to achieve job fulfillment. This involves finding career information, acquiring the right job skills, and marketing our talents through effective resumés, interviews, and networking. Throughout our careers, we will deal with constant job transition as we undergo various job moves, periods of unemployment, and entrepreneurship. The chances of having a successful career will be greater for those who develop leadership, creativity; analytical, problem-solving, and other transferable skills which are useful in an age of information and technology.

Attaining Success and Fulfillment

Each of us wants more and more out of life. We want more out of our job and career than money. We want more out of life than the traditional linear life cycle of going through school, starting a career, raising a family, retiring, and dying. We want a sense of purpose and accomplishment as well as a quality and fulfilling lifestyle.

The U.S. economy grew rapidly during the 1950s and 1960s creating vast opportunities in many areas. Every year we improved our well-being and quality of life. Then through the recessions of the late seventies and eighties, many economic opportunities disappeared; prices, inflation, and unemployment were on the rise; and it became harder to buy a home, save for the future, and pay for college and medical care. Downsizing and job obsolescence because of technological changes also contributed to people's economic problems. In the nineties fulfillment through economic gains will not be reached by many people, and they will look toward non-economic factors to find fulfillment.

The sophisticated population of the 1990s is exploring alternative models of lifestyles and career success. Prior to the "baby boom" generation, people had clearer definitions of success and happiness and a relatively stable model for achieving them. For men, this model was the tradition-oriented "organization man" with family values and strong loyalty to his job. For women, it was primary devotion to home and family—career fulfillment was secondary. Much has changed since the 1950s and, as a result, life in the 1990s is harder to manage and control. This means that alternative ways of satisfying our aspirations will have to be found.

The attributes of career success and quality of worklife will vary for each of us. Although no two people are exactly alike, there are several common areas which are important to quality of worklife. Compensation remains the number one issue affecting quality of worklife for most people. But, employee benefits, such as health care and pensions; job security; flexible work schedules; job stress; profit sharing; fairness; and participation in decision-making are also very important.

We are unwilling, in the nineties, to accept that there are trade-offs between efficiency in a high-tech society and quality of life; we want both. Where previously people found fulfillment through material well-being, they now seek fulfillment through adventure, autonomy, creativity, community involvement, leisure, and endearing relationships. We have shed our ethic of self-denial and now deny nothing in our pursuit of happiness.

Fulfillment through either material or intangible goals will not be attained if there is a mismatch between our goals for fulfillment and our means or willingness to achieve them. We must set challenging, yet realistic, goals for ourselves and learn how to recognize opportunities and avenues for attaining them. Each of us should decide which things are most rewarding to us, and take the time and effort to pursue and enjoy them. We hold the key to our self-fulfillment and inner happiness. We must decide whether a life of mediocrity is acceptable to us. Each of us, whether we choose to follow them or not, have inner drives, visions, and consciousness. Real fulfillment is attained by following our inner selves.

An important part of fulfillment for most people is achieving career success. The responsibility of career management and professional development rests with the individual. Organizations are becoming less and less effective in providing traditional career guidance and growth. Yet, a large number of people are just not prepared technically or mentally to manage their careers—therefore, many will not reach their career expectations. It will be critical that a career self-management program be set up to achieve career success.

Developing a Career Plan

Successful careers generally do not happen by accident. Nor do they happen overnight. Rather, long-range career planning is crucial to attaining career success and fulfillment. Planning helps to define objectives and the means to accomplish them. Great generals, coaches, and leading organizations routinely do it—they would be lost without it. Research has shown that people who plan their careers perform better and are more satisfied with their jobs than those who do not.

It is important that we go through a periodic assessment of ourselves, our skills, and our professional growth and development. We will likely not find success as a jack-of-all-trades and a master of none. Realistically, each of us will probably not consider more than a dozen careers over our lives, but choosing wisely between these will depend on a number of things such as job requirements, occupational characteristics, work environment, our aptitude, skills, talents, goals, objectives, and just plain luck.

Up-to-date career information and effective career counseling can be extremely important in matching personal talents and goals with the demands of a given field of work. Family, friends, instructors, and school associates are a good place to start collecting career and job information. This networking can be valuable in learning about companies, jobs, and career options. It is also a good way to learn about the required training for certain positions, how others in that position entered and advanced, and what they like and dislike about their work. Other sources of information include high school guidance counselors, college placement offices, vocational rehabilitation agencies, state employment service offices, professional associations, and private recruiting and counseling agencies. Remember, that without a thorough understanding of the requirements of available jobs and how jobs at succeeding levels interrelate, effective career planning is impossible.

For maximum flexibility in career planning a person should acquire skills and expertise in at least two fields. Look at strong backgrounds which combine technical, artistic, or specialized skills with business, finance, marketing, or law. Focus on skills which are interchangeable and useful for a variety of occupations, such as leadership, communication, problem-solving, initiative, computer literacy, and teamwork.

We should review our career plans every three to five years to make sure they are on target with where we wanted to be. What adjustments have to be made? Do current positions benefit career goals? If a person must leave an organization, he should try to leave at his convenience and for a better position. To do this requires knowing when it's time to leave and being aware of career opportunities that match long-term career plans.

Our Career Life-Cycles

According to the American Association for Higher Education, most people's careers typically follow some general stages as they progress through life. These stages will vary widely from person to person according to each individual's career clock. With each stage will come constantly changing interests, focuses, and opportunities. The various career stages are also changing because of increasing mobility, shifting technologies, and different priorities between work, family, and leisure. Flexibility and maneuverability will be the ultimate factors in a successful career.

The initial career stage usually occurs in one's early to mid-twenties while pursuing a college education or other professional training and entering the work world. It is at this stage that we typically make our initial decisions about studies, career and a long-term relationship. We make provisional commitments to our occupation and our first job. We fashion an initial life structure and vision of ourselves as a young adult.

Our first job can have a tremendous impact on our early career. Studies have shown that the degree of challenge and satisfaction in our initial job assignments will have a big effect on our performance and progress over the subsequent five to ten years and throughout our career. We should look for an initial job which offers professional stimulation, high visibility, and development of positive relationships.

In our late twenties we are likely to be in a period of transiency. We will probably undergo a host of career and personal events, such as quitting a job, being fired, being unemployed, moving, changing jobs, getting married, and starting a family. We are also likely to find a mentor who will provide some initial career guidance.

In our early thirties we can expect a reexamination of our lives, careers, and other commitments. We are likely to change occupation or career path, and perhaps go back to school. We start to question what life is all about and what we want out of it.

We will likely start to settle down in our mid to late thirties and invest more of ourselves in work, family, and other interests. We become more involved in community and associational activities. We become more accepted as a serious, yet junior, member of our profession, while setting a timetable for achieving concrete, long-range goals. Recognition and job promotions are crucial in confirming our career choices.

Our mid-life transition will likely start in our early forties and continue into our early fifties. We start to restabilize our choices and lifestyle. We will also seek to create a better fit between the world and ourselves. It is important to realize and resolve the differences between our inner self and the realities of our particular circumstances. We will probably take a new look at life ambitions and contemplate a final career change. In fact, it may be imperative to change so that our goals can be accomplished. By this time, we will have become seasoned members of our profession, and we are likely to become mentors and share our knowledge and skills with young associates and friends. Mentoring can be a fulfilling means of making a lasting and significant contribution to one's job or profession. People should also take advantage of opportunities for personal and professional development by attending seminars, workshops, college courses, and other forms of enrichment.

The fact that kids are likely to be grown-up or in college should offer more flexibility and control over our schedule. We can use this time to explore new hobbies and part-time interests. Around age fifty, deferred life goals will probably be revived and vigorously pursued. The transition into the fifties can be a new beginning. From the early to late fifties we will likely accept the status quo, readjust our lives and career goals, and find satisfaction in accomplishments outside the job. We are also likely to go through another restabilization process and acceptance of our particular situations.

In our early sixties we are likely to go through a mellowing of feelings and relationships. We will develop a greater comfort with ourselves and start to define our accomplishments and measurements of success, rather than have others define them for us. Now, more than ever, we start to live for ourselves and not primarily for others. We will likely wind down our careers and prepare for retirement.

Also in our sixties, and beyond, we will probably go through a review of our lives. We will come to accept what has transpired in our lives and realize that it does have worth and meaning. There will typically be an eagerness to share everyday human joys, and our families become a very important focal point.

With each of these stages it is important that we take maximum advantage of each situation, and never lose sight of our long-term career and personal objectives. We must honestly and objectively evaluate ourselves and our performance during each position. We must recognize when we have outstayed our opportunities. We should try not to view a change as an admission of failure, but rather as an honest reflection of our limitations and contributions. Most of all, we must not be afraid of change and new challenges. So many people become too comfortable with their current situation and are paranoid of change. They live their lives in unfulfilling and unrewarding situations merely because circumstances have put them there.

We must be willing to adapt to change and new opportunities as we did as a kid starting kindergarten, or as a young adult getting married and starting a family. Our lives are always in a state of flux and change. Effectively managing that change will make the difference between being happy or miserable. Happiness, success, and fulfillment do not happen by accident.

CHAPTER TWO

THE NEW
JOB MARKET

*N*early twenty million new jobs will be added to the U.S. economy over the next ten years. According to the Bureau of Labor Statistics, total employment will rise from about 128 million in 1994 to about 147 million in the year 2005. This represents an overall job growth of about twenty percent. Employment in jobs requiring a college degree is projected to increase by nearly thirty percent over the same period from about twenty-six million to about thirty-two million. This increase in college-level jobs of nearly six million is less than half of the fourteen to fifteen million new college graduates projected to enter the job market during this time.

Over half of the college-level jobs today and tomorrow will be in professional specialty occupations such as engineering, computer science, chemistry, teaching, and writing. Another thirty percent of the professional jobs will be in executive, administrative, and managerial positions, such as business executives, financial managers, accountants, and education administrators. Close to ten percent will be in sales representative and sales supervisory positions; about five percent will be technicians; and the remaining five percent will be in areas such as law enforcement and miscellaneous supervisory and administrative support.

The Future Job Outlook

The future demand for college graduates and non-graduates will be determined by factors such as the rate of economic and industrial growth, the growth of occupations caused by changes in technology and business practices, increasing complexity of specific occupations, and the need to replace workers because of attrition. Most of the new jobs over the next ten to fifteen years will fall within the professional specialty, executive, administrative, and managerial areas.

The impact of more college graduates entering the labor force than there will be professional job openings means that some people will not find college-level jobs. Those who select their career carefully, acquire the appropriate educational background, and market their abilities well are likely to have the best chances of success. Others will have to scramble for the available jobs. They risk periods of unemployment, may have to accept jobs that do not require their level of education, or hop from job to job before finding a satisfying position.

College graduates who are underutilized will crowd out others who would normally fill jobs requiring less than a college education. This means that noncollege graduates will also need to plan their careers carefully. Those who prepare themselves for jobs requiring specific skills, such as a bookkeeper or technician, will do much better than those who lack specialized training.

It is important that both college graduates and others know which occupations are likely to offer the best employment prospects. Every two years, the U.S. Department of Labor, Bureau of Labor Statistics develops projections of the labor force, economic growth, industry output and occupational employment. These projections typically cover a ten- to fifteen-year period and the information on employment trends in approximately 250 occupations are listed in the *Occupational Outlook Handbook* (available from the Superintendent of Documents, U.S. Government Printing Office, Washington, D.C. 20402). Information from the 1992 *Handbook* on many occupations in the executive, managerial, administrative, professional specialty, technician, marketing, sales, clerical and service areas are reprinted later in this chapter covering the time period from 1990 to 2005.

Jobs in the executive, administrative, and managerial areas typically involve establishing policies, planning, staffing, and directing the activities of businesses, government agencies and other organizations. Because of the increasing complexity and overall expansion in business and economic activities, jobs in this area will grow faster than average for 1990 to 2005. Occupations in this area which will show the most growth, about thirty percent or more, include: accountants and auditors; construction managers; managers of engineering, science, and data processing; financial managers; health services managers; hotel managers; inspectors and compliance officers; management analysts and consultants; marketing, advertising, and public relations managers; personnel managers; property and real estate managers; and restaurant and food service managers. The best paying jobs in this category are in the marketing and financial areas. People with work experience, specialized training, graduate study, and familiarity with computers will have an advantage in filling these positions.

Professional specialty occupations are also expected to grow faster than average and significantly increase their share of total employment by 2005. The biggest growth in this area will come in engineering—especially civil and electrical; landscape architects; actuaries; computer systems analysts; operations research analysts; biological scientists; lawyers and judges; psychologists; secondary school teachers; physicians; podiatrists; veterinarians; physical therapists; registered nurses; respiratory therapists; and graphic artists. Physicians, lawyers, engineers, computer systems analysts, scientists, and nurses will enjoy the highest salaries in this area.

Technicians and related support-occupations involve operating and programming technical equipment and assisting engineers, scientists, health practitioners, and other professionals.

Overall employment in this area is expected to grow faster than any of the other major occupational groups, with tremendous growth in jobs for paralegals, computer programmers, licensed practical nurses, and medical-related technologists.

Marketing and sales will show only an average overall growth during the next ten years, although jobs for financial, travel, and service sales-representatives will increase about forty to sixty percent. Job opportunities will be best for well-trained, personable, and ambitious people who enjoy selling. The best compensation will be in manufacturing, mining, and wholesale sales.

Service occupations include a wide variety of jobs in protective service, food preparation, health service, and personal service. The growing population and economy, higher personal incomes, and increased leisure time will contribute to above average growth here. Jobs as correction officers, medical assistants, and nursing aides are the most promising.

Occupational Profiles for 1990–2005

Occupational profiles for 1990 to 2005 from *Occupational Outlook Quarterly,* Spring 1992 are listed below. These profiles provide useful information on current employment in a substantial number of jobs, percent change and total new jobs up to 2005, and employment prospects for the future.

Occupational Profiles for 1990–2005

(Source: *Occupational Outlook Quarterly,* Spring 1992)

Occupation	Estimated employment 1990	Percent change in employment 1990–2005	Numerical change in employment 1990–2005	Employment prospects
EXECUTIVE, ADMINISTRATIVE, AND MANAGERIAL OCCUPATIONS				
Accountants	985,000	34	340,000	As the number of businesses increases and audits and the complexity of the financial information required grow, more accountants and auditors will be needed to set up books, prepare taxes and advise management. Faster than average job growth is expected which should result in favorable opportunities for those with a bachelor's or higher degree in accounting.

Occupation	Estimated employment 1990	Percent change in employment 1990–2005	Numerical change in employment 1990–2005	Employment prospects
Administrative service managers	221,000	23	52,000	Average employment growth is expected. Although demand should be spurred by the growing need for various administrative services—overseeing the implementation and operation of sophisticated office systems, for example—corporate attempts to reduce administrative costs by streamlining office and information handling procedures will offset the increase in demand. As with other managerial jobs, the ample supply of competent, experienced workers seeking advancement should result in competition for these jobs.
Budget analysts	64,000	22	14,000	Although the increasing use of automation may make budget analysts more productive, the growing complexity of business and increasing need for information will result in average employment growth. Keen competition for jobs is expected; prospects will be best for holders of a master's degree and college graduates with experience in finance and accounting.
Construction and building inspectors	60,000	19	11,000	Increases in the level and complexity of construction activity, rising concern for public safety, and growing desire for improvements in the quality of construction should result in average employment growth. Job prospects will be best for experienced craft workers who have some college education or are certified.
Construction contractors and managers	183,000	33	60,000	Increases in the size and complexity of construction projects and the proliferation of laws setting standards for buildings and construction materials, worker safety, energy efficiency, and pollution should result in faster than average growth. Completion of a bachelor's degree program in construction science with emphasis on construction management can greatly enhance one's opportunities in this field.
Cost estimators	173,000	24	42,000	Average growth is expected as more estimators are needed to predict the cost of the growing number of construction and manufacturing projects. In construction, job prospects will be best for those with construction experience or with a degree in construction management, engineering, or architectural drafting; in manufacturing, job prospects will be best for experienced people with computer expertise and a degree in engineering, science, math, business, or economics.
Education administrators	348,000	24	85,000	Employment is expected to grow as fast as average as school enrollments increase. Substantial competition is expected for principal, assistant principal, and central office jobs because many teachers and other staff meet the requirements for these jobs and seek promotion.

29

Occupation	Estimated employment 1990	Percent change in employment 1990–2005	Numerical change in employment 1990–2005	Employment prospects
Employment interviewers	83,000	23	19,000	Average growth is expected due to the expansion of employment agencies and temporary help firms. Opportunities should be excellent for articulate, outgoing people who enjoy public contact and a fast-paced work environment.
Engineering, science, and processing managers	315,000	34	108,000	Faster than average employment growth is expected. Employment growth of each type of manager is data expected to correspond closely with growth of the occupation supervised.
Financial managers	701,000	28	193,000	The need for sound financial advice should spur faster than average growth for several reasons: The increasing variety and complexity of financial service, increased interstate and international banking, growing competition, changing laws regarding taxes and other financial matters, and greater emphasis on the accuracy of financial data. As in other management occupations, applicants face competition for positions; opportunities will be best for those familiar with data processing and management information systems and a wide range of financial services.
General managers and top executives	3,086,000	19	598,000	Expansion in the size, number, and complexity of business firms should spur demand for general managers and top executives. However, many firms are improving operating efficiency by establishing a leaner corporate structure with fewer management positions, resulting in average employment growth. Substantial competition is expected for these high paying, prestigious jobs due to the number of lower level managers seeking advancement.
Health service managers	257,000	42	108,000	Much faster than average growth is expected as the health care industry expands and diversifies. Employment in home health care services and nursing care facilities will grow the fastest.
Hotel managers and assistants	102,000	44	45,000	The growing volume of business and vacation travel will increase demand for hotels and motels, spurring much faster than average growth. Opportunities should be best for people with college degrees in hotel or restaurant management.
Industrial production managers	210,000	20	41,000	Average employment growth will be fueled by increased production of consumer and industrial products. Prospects will be best for those who have a master's degree in business administration, especially if they also have an undergraduate degree in engineering.
Inspectors and compliance	156,000	30	46,000	Faster than average employment growth will be spurred by expansion of regulatory and compliance

Occupation	Estimated employment 1990	Percent change in employment 1990-2005	Numerical change in employment 1990-2005	Employment prospects
officers except construction				programs in government, especially in local government, and by increasing self-enforcement of government regulations and company policies in private industry.
Management analysts and consultants	151,000	52	79,000	Competitive pressures on organizations will contribute to much faster than average growth. Opportunities will be best for those with a graduate degree or industry expertise. Good organizational and marketing skills, plus several years of consulting experience, are essential for people interested in starting their own firm.
Marketing, advertising, and public relations managers	427,000	47	203,000	Intensifying domestic and foreign competition—requiring greater marketing, promotional, and public relations efforts—should result in much faster than average growth. However, these jobs will be sought by other managers and experienced professional and technical personnel, resulting in substantial competition. Job prospects will be best for experienced, creative college graduates who communicate well.
Personnel, training, and labor relations specialists and managers	456,000	32	144,000	Faster than average growth is expected as employers devote greater resources to training programs in response to the increasing complexity of many jobs, the aging of the work force, and advances in technology that can leave employees with obsolete skills. Also, legislation and court rulings setting standards in occupational safety and health, equal employment opportunity, employment benefits, and other areas has increased the amount of recordkeeping, analysis, and report writing required. However, the job market is likely to remain competitive in view of the abundant supply of college graduates and experienced workers with suitable qualifications.
Property and real estate managers	225,000	34	76,000	Faster than average job growth is expected to result from increases in the number of office buildings, retail properties, and apartment complexes requiring management. Overbuilding and the subsequent concern for profitable property management should also stimulate employment growth. People with a college degree in business administration or a related field should have the best job opportunities.
Purchasing agents and managers	300,000	23	69,000	The increased recognition of the importance of efficient purchasing procedures is expected to result in average growth. Those with a bachelor's or advanced degree should have the best opportunities.
Restaurant and food service managers	556,000	32	177,000	Growth in the number of eating and drinking establishments will result in faster than average growth in employment. Opportunities are expected to be best

Occupation	Estimated employment 1990	Percent change in employment 1990–2005	Numerical change in employment 1990–2005	Employment prospects
				for people with degrees in restaurant or institutional food service management.
Underwriters	105,000	24	25,000	Employment is expected to grow as fast as average. The expected rise in the volume, complexity, and variety of insurance products will be offset by the trend toward self insurance and the increased use of artificial intelligence. Underwriters with extensive computer knowledge should have the best opportunities.
Wholesale and retail buyers and merchandise managers	361,000	19	68,000	Although sales volume will continue to increase, the centralization of purchasing departments will result in only average growth. Because merchandising attracts many college graduates, applicants are likely to continue to be more numerous than openings. Job prospects will be best for those with previous wholesale or retail experience.

PROFESSIONAL SPECIALTY OCCUPATIONS

Occupation	Estimated employment 1990	Percent change in employment 1990–2005	Numerical change in employment 1990–2005	Employment prospects
Engineers	1,519,000	26	400,000	Opportunities for those with degrees in engineering have been good since the mid-1970s, and this trend is expected to continue. Employment of engineers is expected to increase faster than average. Much of the growth will stem from higher levels of investment in industrial plants and equipment to meet the demand for more goods and services and to increase productivity.
Aerospace engineers	73,000	20	15,000	Although defense expenditures for military aircraft, missiles, and other aerospace systems are expected to decline, employment is expected to increase about as fast as average because of growth in the civilian sector. Many commercial planes will be replaced with quieter, more fuel-efficient aircraft, and increased demand for spacecraft, helicopters, and business aircraft is expected.
Chemical engineers	45,000	12	5,600	Employment will grow more slowly than average—because little, if any, growth is expected in the chemical manufacturing industry, where many chemical engineers are employed. Industrial chemicals, biotechnology, and materials science may provide better opportunities than other portions of the chemical industry.
Civil engineers	198,000	30	59,000	A growing population and economy—and the result ing need to design, construct, and rebuild transportation systems, water resource and disposal systems, large buildings, and other structures—should result in faster than average growth.
Electrical and electronics engineers	426,000	34	145,000	Increased demand for computers, electronic consmer goods, communications equipment, and other electrical and electronic products is expected to result in

Occupation	Estimated employment 1990	Percent change in employment 1990–2005	Numerical change in employment 1990–2005	Employment prospects
				faster than average growth. Opportunities should be favorable.
Industrial engineers	135,000	19	26,000	Employment is expected to grow about as fast as average due to the increased complexity of business operations, increased interest in efficiency by businesses, and greater use of automation in factories and offices. Qualified applicants should find good job prospects.
Mechanical engineers	233,000	24	56,000	Average growth is expected as the demand for machinery and machine tools grows and as industrial machinery and processes become increasingly complex. Because mechanical engineering is the broadest engineering discipline, opportunities should be favorable in many industries.
Metallurgical, ceramic, and materials engineers	18,000	21	3,900	Employment should increase about as fast as average to meet the demands on metalworking and other industries to develop new materials and to adapt existing ones to new applications.
Architects and surveyors				
Architects	108,000	24	26,000	Good opportunities are expected because employment growth should be as fast as average and because the number of degrees granted in architecture is not expected to increase significantly. Competition will continue for jobs in the most prestigious firms, as well as during recessions or slowdowns in construction.
Landscape architects	20,000	31	6,200	Growth in new construction over the long run and a growing commitment to environmental planning and historic preservation will result in faster than average growth.
Surveyors	108,000	14	15,000	Increased real estate transactions and construction should contribute to average growth. However, employment fluctuates from year to year because construction is sensitive to changes in economic conditions. The best opportunities will be for those with at least a bachelor's degree.
Computer, mathematical, and operations research occupations				
Actuaries	13,000	34	4,400	Faster than average employment growth will be spurred by the increasing volume and complexity of insurance policies and health and pension plans and by the introduction of new forms of insurance. Actuaries may face competition for jobs because the number of workers entering the occupation has increased substantially in recent years. Opportunities will be best for college graduates who have passed at least two

33

Occupation	Estimated employment 1990	Percent change in employment 1990-2005	Numerical change in employment 1990-2005	Employment prospects
				actuarial exams while still in school and have a strong background in mathematics and statistics.
Computer systems analysts	463,000	79	366,000	Employment is expected to grow much faster than average as organizations attempt to maximize efficiency by networking their computer systems for office and factory automation, communications capability, and scientific research. Job prospects will be very good for college graduates who combine courses in programming and systems analysis with training and experience in applied fields.
Mathematicians	22,000	9	2,000	Employment is expected to grow more slowly than average. However, the continuing shortage of Ph.Ds will result in favorable opportunities for mathematicians, especially those with doctorates in applied mathematics. Those with a master's or bachelor's degree who have strong backgrounds in computer science, electrical or mechanical engineering, or operations research should also have good job opportunities.
Operations research analysts	57,000	73	42,000	As computer costs fall and competitive pressures grow, more organizations will turn to operations research to aid decision-making, resulting in much faster than average growth. Opportunities will be especially favorable in manufacturing, trade, and service firms.
Statisticians	16,000	12	18,00	Although employment is expected to grow more slowly than average, job opportunities should remain favorable, especially for people with advanced degrees. Graduates with a bachelor's degree in statistics and a strong background in mathematics or computer science should have the best prospects of finding jobs related to their field of study.
Life scientists				
Agricultural scientists	25,000	27	6,600	Good employment prospects are expected because enrollments in agricultural science curriculums have dropped considerably over the last few years and because employment should grow faster than average. Animal and plant scientists with a background in molecular biology, microbiology, genetics, or biotechnology; soil scientists; and food technologists will probably have the best opportunities.
Biological scientists	62,000	34	21,000	Increased demand for genetic and biological research, in part because of efforts to preserve and clean up the environment, should result in faster than average growth. Most new jobs will be in the private sector; employment in government is expected to grow slowly.

Occupation	Estimated employment 1990	Percent change in employment 1990–2005	Numerical change in employment 1990–2005	Employment prospects
Foresters and conservation scientists	29,000	12	3,600	Budgetary constraints in government, where employment is highly concentrated, will result in slower than average overall growth. However, state governments and private owners of timberland may employ more foresters due to increased interest in environmental protection and land management. Overall, job opportunities should be more favorable than in the past due to an expected wave of retirements and recent declines in the number of graduates in forestry and related fields.
Physical scientists				
Chemists	83,000	16	13,000	Very good employment opportunities are expected because the number of graduates with degrees in chemistry is not expected to increase enough to meet future demand. Employment should increase about as fast as average. Job opportunities will be best in pharmaceuticals and biotechnology, where Ph.D. chemists are expected to be in strong demand.
Geologists and geophysicists	48,000	22	11,000	Environmental protection and regulation are becoming important fields of work for those with the appropriate training. When oil and gas exploration activities increase, geologists and geophysicists should have excellent opportunities. Average growth is expected.
Social scientists and urban planners				
Economists and marketing research analysts	37,000	21	8,000	Employment is expected to increase as fast as average, reflecting increased reliance on quantitative methods to analyze business trends, forecast sales, and plan purchasing and production. For economists, master's and doctoral degree holders will have the best opportunities. Bachelor's degree holders face competition; those skilled in quantitative techniques have the best prospects. For marketing research positions, those with an advanced degree in marketing or a related field have the best prospects.
Lawyers and judges	633,000	34	217,000	The demand for legal services caused by population growth and economic expansion will create faster than average employment growth. Competition is expected to ease somewhat for salaried attorney positions, but remain intense for judgeships.
Psychologists	125,000	64	79,000	Much faster than average growth is anticipated due to increased attention being paid to the expanding elderly population, the maintenance of mental health, and the testing and counseling of children. Ph.D.s with training in applied areas, such as clinical or counseling psychology, and in quantitative research methods will have the best prospects. Among master's degree

Occupation	Estimated employment 1990	Percent change in employment 1990-2005	Numerical change in employment 1990-2005	Employment prospects
				holders, specialists in school psychology should have the best prospects, while bachelor's degree holders will have very few opportunities in this field.
Urban and regional planners	23,000	19	4,400	Increased demand for planning related to the environment, the economy, transportation, and energy production should result in average employment growth. Opportunities will be best in rapidly growing areas, older areas undergoing preservation and redevelopment, and states that have mandated planning. Graduates of institutions with accredited planning programs have the best prospects.

Teachers, librarians, and counselors

Occupation	Estimated employment 1990	Percent change in employment 1990-2005	Numerical change in employment 1990-2005	Employment prospects
Adult education teachers	517,000	29	152,000	Overall employment is expected to grow faster than average as demand for adult education programs continues to rise. Many openings will arise from the need to replace workers who leave the occupation, particularly given the large number of part-time workers and high turnover in the occupation.
Archivists and curators	17,000	21	3,700	Employment will increase as fast as average, continuing past trends. Competition for jobs will remain keen, however, given the small number of job openings and large supply of workers.
College and university faculty	712,000	19	134,000	Average employment growth is expected as enrollments increase. Beginning in the late 1990s, job opportunities should improve due to an expected wave of faculty retirements. Job prospects are best with business, engineering, computer, and science faculties because of the availability of high-paying jobs outside academia.
Counselors	144,000	23	350,000	Employment is expected to grow faster than average, due to increasing school enrollments, greater use of third party payments to counselors, and the expanded responsibilities of counselors. Job openings should increase by the year 2005 as the large number of counselors now in their forties and fifties reach retirement age.
Kindergarten and elementary school teachers	1,521,000	23	350,000	Average employment growth is expected as enrollments increase and class size declines. The number of job openings should increase substantially after the mid-1990s, as the large number of teachers now in their forties and fifties reach retirement age.
Librarians	149,000	11	17,000	Employment is expected to grow more slowly than average, continuing the limited employment growth of librarians during the 1980s. The decline in the number of graduates of library science programs in the 1980s,

Occupation	Estimated employment 1990	Percent change in employment 1990–2005	Numerical change in employment 1990–2005	Employment prospects
				however, should result in favorable job prospects for such graduates.
Secondary school teachers	1,280,000	34	437,000	Employment is expected to increase faster than average as enrollments grow and class size declines. Job openings will increase substantially after the mid-1990s as the large number of teachers now in their forties and fifties reach retirement age.
Health diagnosing occupations				
Dentists	174,000	12	21,000	Job prospects should continue to improve because the number of dental school graduates has declined since the early 1980s and is not likely to increase much. Despite a growing demand for dental services, employment is projected to grown more slowly than average. Dentists should respond to growing demand by working more hours and relying on dental hygienists and assistants to provide more services.
Optometrists	37,000	20	7,600	Employment is expected to grow as fast as average in order to meet the needs of a population that is larger, older, and more aware of the need for proper eye care. Job opportunities should be good, even though replacement needs are low.
Physicians	580,000	34	196,000	Employment is expected to grown faster than average due to a growing and aging population and technological improvements that encourage expansion of the health industry. Job prospects should be better in internal medicine, family practice, geriatrics, and preventive medicine than in other specialties.
Podiatrists	16,000	46	7,300	Employment is expected to grow much faster than average due to the rising demand for podiatric services, in particular by older people and fitness enthusiasts. Establishing a new podiatric practice will be toughest in areas surrounding the seven colleges of podiatric medicine since podiatrists are concentrated in these locations.
Veterinarians	47,000	31	14,000	Employment is expected to grow faster than average due to growth in the animal population and the willingness of pet owners to pay for more intensive care than in the past. The outlook for specialists—such as toxicologists, laboratory veterinarians, and pathologists—will be extremely good.
Health assessment and treating occupations				
Dietitians and nutritionists	45,000	24	11,000	Employment is expected to grow about as fast as average in order to meet the expanding needs of nursing homes, hospitals, and social service programs

37

Occupation	Estimated employment 1990	Percent change in employment 1990–2005	Numerical change in employment 1990–2005	Employment prospects
				and the growing interest and emphasis on dietary education.
Occupational therapists	36,000	55	20,000	Much faster than average growth is expected, reflecting anticipated growth in demand for rehabilitation services due to the increased survival rate of accident victims and the rising number of people in their forties, an age when the risk of heart disease and stroke increases. The rapidly growing aged population will also increase demand for long-term care services. In addition, therapists will be needed for disabled students.
Pharmacists	169,000	21	35,000	Spurred by the pharmaceutical needs of a larger and older population and by scientific advances that will bring more drugs onto the market, employment is expected to grow as fast as average. Excellent job prospects are anticipated in both community and clinical settings; if current trends continue, demand is likely to outstrip supply in some places.
Physical therapists	88,000	76	67,000	Much faster than average job growth is expected due to the expansion of services for those in need of rehabilitation and long-term care. The shortage of physical therapists should ease somewhat as the number of physical therapy education programs increases and more students graduate.
Physician assistants	53,000	34	18,000	Employment is expected to grow faster than average due to the expansion of the health services industry and the increased emphasis on cost containment. Excellent prospects are anticipated, especially in areas that have difficulty attracting physicians.
Recreational therapists	32,000	39	13,000	Employment is expected to grow much faster than average, chiefly because of anticipated growth in the need for long-term care, rehabilitation, and services for the developmentally disabled. Job prospects should be favorable for those with a strong clinical background.
Registered nurses	1,727,000	44	767,000	Much faster than average growth is expected, due to the overall growth in health care and the number of complex medical technologies. Hospitals in many parts of the country report shortages of RNs. However, increasing enrollments in nursing programs may result in a balance between job seekers and openings.
Respiratory therapists	60,000	52	31,000	Much faster than average growth is expected be cause of the substantial growth of the middle-aged and elderly population, which is more likely to suffer from cardiopulmonary diseases. Hospitals will continue to be the primary employer, but employment will grow fastest in home health care services.

Occupation	Estimated employment 1990	Percent change in employment 1990-2005	Numerical change in employment 1990-2005	Employment prospects
Speech-language pathologists and audiologists	68,000	34	23,000	Faster than average overall growth is expected, but the rate varies by industry. Much faster than average growth is likely in the health care industry because the number of older people will grow rapidly and the baby-boom generation will enter an age bracket when the possibility of stroke-induced hearing and speed loss increases. Average growth is expected in educational services.

Communications occupations

Public relations ists	109,000	19	21,000	Average growth is expected as organizations increasingly recognize the need for good internal and special-external relations. Keen competition for these jobs is likely to persist among recent college graduates with communications degrees; people without the appropriate education or experience will face the toughest obstacles in acquiring these jobs.
Radio and TV announcers and newscasters	57,000	20	11,000	Average growth is expected as new radio and TV stations are licensed and the number of cable TV stations continues to grow. Competition for begin ning jobs will be very strong because the broadcasting field attracts many more jobseekers than there are jobs. Jobs will be easier to find in radio than in TV because more radio stations hire beginners.
Reporters and correspondents	67,000	20	14,000	Employment is expected to grow about as fast as average. Writers who can handle highly specialized scientific or technical subjects will be at an advantage in the job market. The best opportunities are likely to be found on newspapers and magazines in small towns and suburbs.
Writers and editors	232,000	26	60,000	Increased demand for salaried writers in publishing, public relations, communications, and advertising should cause employment to rise faster than average. Keen competition is expected to continue. Opportunities will be best with business, trade, and technical publications.

Visual arts occupations

Designers	339,000	26	89,000	Continued emphasis on the quality and visual appeal of products will prompt faster than average growth for designers, especially industrial designers. Designers in most specialties will face competition throughout their careers because of the abundant supply of talented, highly qualified people attracted to this field. Finding a job in floral design should be relatively easy due to the relatively low pay and limited advancement opportunities.

Occupation	Estimated employment 1990	Percent change in employment 1990–2005	Numerical change in employment 1990–2005	Employment prospects
Photographers and camera operators	120,000	23	28,000	Average overall growth is expected in response to the growing importance of visual images in education, communications, and entertainment. Faster than average growth is expected for camera operators. Job seekers may face competition or keen competition, especially in commercial photography and photojournalism.
Visual artists	230,000	32	73,000	Strong demand for art, illustration, and design by advertising agencies, publishing firms, and other businesses will stimulate faster than average growth for graphic artists. Competition for jobs among fine artists will continue to be keen.

Performing arts occupations

Occupation	Estimated employment 1990	Percent change in employment 1990–2005	Numerical change in employment 1990–2005	Employment prospects
Actors, directors, and producers	95,000	41	39,000	Employment is expected to grow much faster than average as cable television, home movie rentals, and television syndication fuel a growing demand for productions. Still, continued overcrowding in this field will cause keen competition for jobs.
Dancers and choreographers	8,600	38	3,300	Employment is expected to grow much faster than average. Nonetheless, dancers seeking professional careers will continue to exceed the number of job openings, causing keen competition.
Musicians	252,000	9	24,000	Employment is expected to grown more slowly than average, reflecting the increasing use of synthesizers instead of multi-piece bands and orchestras. Also, a growing number of small clubs and dining establishments are hiring smaller bands than they have in the past. Competition will be extremely keen.

TECHNICIANS AND RELATED SUPPORT OCCUPATIONS

Health technologists and technicians

Occupation	Estimated employment 1990	Percent change in employment 1990–2005	Numerical change in employment 1990–2005	Employment prospects
Clinical laboratory technicians	258,000	24	63,000	Although the number of medical tests will greatly increase, advances in laboratory automation should boost productivity, resulting in average employment growth. Many jobs will be in hospitals, but the fastest growth will be in commercial laboratories and doctors' offices due to changes in technology and business strategy. Job prospects are favorable.
Dental hygienists	97,000	41	40,000	Employment should grow much faster than average. Stimulating demand will be population growth, the tendency for middle-aged and elderly people to retain their teeth, and greater awareness of the importance of dental care along with the ability to pay for it. Also, dentists are expected to rely on hygienists to provide more services. Dental hygienists should have little trouble finding jobs.

Occupation	Estimated employment 1990	Percent change in employment 1990–2005	Numerical change in employment 1990–2005	Employment prospects
Dispensing opticians	64,000	37	24,000	Employment is expected to grow much faster than average in response to rising demand for corrective lenses as the population ages. Opportunities should be very good for graduates of formal training programs.
EEG technologists	6,700	57	3,800	Much faster than average growth is expected, reflecting the increased numbers of neurodiagnostic tests performed. Job prospects should be excellent for formally trained technologists.
EKG technicians	16,000	–5	–800	Employment is expected to decline, despite the anticipated rise in the number of cardiology tests performed. Advances in technology have substantially raised EKG technicians' productivity and also have allowed registered nurses and other health personnel to perform the test.
Emergency medical technicians	89,000	30	26,000	Faster than average job growth is projected. Opportunities should be excellent in hospitals and private ambulance services, where pay and benefits generally are low. Competition will be keen in fire, police, and rescue squads because of attractive pay and benefits and good job security.
Licensed pratical nurses	644,000	42	269,000	Employment is expected to grow much faster than average in response to the long-term care needs of a rapidly growing aged population and growth in health care in general. The job outlook should remain good unless the number of people completing L.P.N. training increases substantially.
Medical record technicians	52,000	54	28,000	Greater use of medical records for financial management and quality control will produce much faster than average job growth with excellent job prospects for graduates of accredited programs in medical record technology.
Nuclear medicine technologists	10,000	53	5,500	Employment is expected to grow much faster than average to meet the health care needs of a growing and aging population. Technological innovations will also increase the diagnostic use of nuclear medicine. Job prospects are excellent.
Radiologic technologists	149,000	70	103,000	Employment is expected to grow much faster than average due to the growth and aging of the population and the greater role radiologic technologies are playing in the diagnosis and treatment of disease. Job prospects for graduates of accredited programs are excellent.
Surgical technologists	38,000	55	21,000	Much faster than average growth is expected as a growing population and technological advances increase the number of surgical procedures per-

Occupation	Estimated employment 1990	Percent change in employment 1990–2005	Numerical change in employment 1990–2005	Employment prospects
				formed. Growth will be fastest in clinics and offices of physicians due to increases in outpatient surgery; however, most jobs will be in hospitals.
Technicians except health				
Aircraft pilots	90,000	34	31,000	Due to an expected shortage of qualified applicants, opportunities should be excellent in the coming years. Faster than average employment growth and the large number of expected retirements will provide many job openings. Job prospects with major airlines are best for college graduates who have a commercial pilot's license or a flight engineer's license and experience flying jets.
Air traffic controllers	32,000	7	2,200	Despite growth in the number of aircraft in service, productivity gains stemming from laborsaving air traffic control equipment will result in slower than average employment growth. Keen competition for job openings is expected because the occupation's relatively high pay and liberal retirement program attract many applicants.
Broadcast technicians	33,000	4	1,200	Because of laborsaving advances, such as computer-controlled programming and remote-controlled transmitters, employment is expected to show little or no change.
Computer programmers	565,000	56	317,000	Employment is expected to grow much faster than average as the number of computer applications continues to increase. Job prospects will be best for college graduates who majored in computer science or a related area and have experience or training in fields such as accounting, management, engineering, or science.
Drafters	326,000	13	44,000	Although large increases in demand for drafting services are expected, they will be partially offset by the widespread use of computer-aided design equipment, which increases the productivity of drafters. Slower than average employment growth is expected.
Engineering technicians	755,000	28	210,000	Well-qualified engineering technicians should experience good opportunities. Anticipated increases in spending on research and development and continued rapid growth in the number of technical products are expected to result in faster than average growth.
Library technicians	65,000	11	7,300	Employment is expected to grow more slowly than average, following the growth pattern of other library workers.
Paralegals	90,000	85	77,000	Much faster than average growth is expected as the

Occupation	Estimated employment 1990	Percent change in employment 1990-2005	Numerical change in employment 1990-2005	Employment prospects
				use of paralegals to aid lawyers increases. Competition for jobs is expected to increase. Opportunities will be best for graduates of well regarded formal paralegal training programs and paralegals with previous experience.
Science technicians	246,000	24	58,000	Science technicians with good technical and commu nication skills should experience very good employ ment opportunities. Expansion in research, development, and the production of technical products will result in average overall growth. The employment and biological technicians is expected to grow faster than most other science technicians; job opportunities for chemical technicians also are expected to be good.
Tool programmers, numerical control	7,800	6	500	Despite increased use of numerically controlled machine tools, employment will grow more slowly than average due to expected large increases in productivity.

MARKETING AND SALES OCCUPATIONS

Occupation	Estimated employment 1990	Percent change	Numerical change	Employment prospects
Cashiers	2,633,000	26	685,000	Faster than average growth is expected due to the anticipated increase in retail sales and the popularity of discount and self-service retailing, which has led to the rise of centralized cashier stations. Due to the large size of this occupation and its much higher than average turnover, both part- and full-time job opportunities will be excellent.
Counter and rental clerks	215,000	34	74,000	Faster than average employment growth is expected due to the anticipated growth in rental and leasing services. Prospects for full- and part-time jobs with flexible hours are excellent.
Insurance agents and brokers	439,000	20	88,000	Due to increasing productivity and changing business practices, employment growth will not keep pace with rising insurance sales, but it will still be as fast as average. Many beginners cannot establish a sufficient clientele in this highly competitive business. Opportunities will be best for ambitious people who enjoy selling and develop expertise in a wide range of insurance and financial services.
Manufacturers' wholesale sales representatives	1,944,000	15	284,000	Average employment growth is expected as the and economy expands and as demand for goods increases. Job prospects will be good for qualified persons.
Real estate agents, brokers and appraisers	413,000	19	79,000	The large proportion of the population between the ages of twenty-five and fifty-four is expected to increase sales of residential and commercial properties, resulting in average employment growth. Because turnover is high, positions should continue to be

43

Occupation	Estimated employment 1990	Percent change in employment 1990–2005	Numerical change in employment 1990–2005	Employment prospects
				relatively easy to obtain. Well-trained, ambitious people who enjoy selling have the best chance for success in this highly competitive field.
Retail sales workers	4,754,000	29	1,381,000	Employment is expected to grow faster than average due to anticipated growth in retail sales. Job prospects will be excellent for full-time, part-time, and temporary workers.
Securities and financial services sales representatives	191,000	40	76,000	Employment is expected to grow much faster than average as economic growth and rising personal incomes increase the funds available for investment and as banks and other financial institutions offer an increasing array of financial services. However, job competition will remain keen, particularly in large firms, due to the potential for high earnings. Many beginners leave securities sales jobs because they are unable to establish a sufficient clientele.
Services sales representative	588,000	55	325,000	The continued rapid increase in the demand for services will result in much faster than average employment growth. Applicants with college training or a proven sales record have the best job prospects.
Travel agents	132,000	62	82,000	Much faster than average employment growth is projected due to the large increases expected in both vacation and business-related travel.

SERVICE OCCUPATIONS

Protective service occupations

Occupation	Estimated employment 1990	Percent change	Numerical change	Employment prospects
Correction officers	230,000	61	142,000	As correctional facilities expand and additional officers are hired to supervise and counsel a growing number of inmates, employment is expected to increase much faster than average. Rapid growth in demand coupled with job openings resulting from turnover should mean favorable opportunities.
Firefighting occupations	280,000	24	68,000	Due to population growth and the increasing need for protection from fires, employment will grow about as fast as average. Keen competition is expected in most areas; the best opportunities are likely to be found in smaller communities with expanding populations.
Guards	883,000	34	298,000	Increasing concern about crime, vandalism, and terrorism will stimulate the need for guards, resulting in faster than average growth. Overall, job opportunities are expected to be plentiful. Opportunities will be best for those who work for contract security agencies. Some competition is expected for in-house guard jobs, which generally have higher salaries, more benefits, better job security, and greater potential for advancement.

Occupation	Estimated employment 1990	Percent change in employment 1990–2005	Numerical change in employment 1990–2005	Employment prospects
Police, detectives, and special agents	655,000	24	160,000	Employment is expected to rise about as fast as average due to an increase in the population, the need for police protection, and the growing concern about drugs and drug-related crimes. Keen competition is expected for higher paying jobs in large police departments and Federal law enforcement agencies, such as the FBI, Drug Enforcement Administration, and the Secret Service.
Health service occupations				
Dental assistants	176,000	34	60,000	Faster than average growth is expected as demand for dental care increases in response to population growth, greater retention of natural teeth by the middle-aged and older population, and greater ability to pay for services. Also, dentists are expected to rely on assistants to provide more services.
Medical assistants	165,000	74	122,000	Much faster than average growth is anticipated due to expansion of the health services industry. Job opportunities should be very good. Most job openings will result from replacement needs.
Nursing aides and psychiatric aides	1,374,000	43	587,000	Job prospects are expected to be very good. Overall employment is projected to grow much faster than average. Employment of nursing aides will grow much faster than average as a result of the anticipated expansion of nursing and personal care facilities. Employment of psychiatric aides is expected to grow faster than average in response to the needs of the very old and those suffering from acute psychiatric and substance abuse problems. Replacement needs will be high.

Tomorrow's Job Earnings

Compensation continues to be a major factor affecting career choices. Even people looking for job satisfaction in other ways will welcome good salaries. Earnings vary widely between occupations, with lawyers and physicians averaging nearly $60,000 a year and food service workers earning about $16,000 annually. There are also large differences in starting salaries for new college graduates depending on their area of study. Generally, graduates with degrees in chemical, mechanical and electrical engineering, and computer science will have the highest starting salaries ranging from about $33,000–35,000 yearly.

Listed below are ranges for the 1994 estimated median annual earnings for over thirty common occupations and the estimated starting salaries for 1994 graduates with bachelor's degrees in fourteen major areas of study.

Estimated Median Annual Earnings for 1994*

	4 years of college	5+ years of college
Executive, administrative, and managerial occupations		
Financial managers	$41–43,000	$51–53,000
Marketing, advertising, and public relations managers	49–51,000	57–59,000
Properties and real estate managers	34–36,000	—
Accountants and auditors	32–34,000	40–42,000
Personnel, training, and labor relations specialists	33–35,000	43–45,000
Purchasing agents and buyers	33–35,000	—
Professional specialty occupations		
Engineers	$44–47,000	$51–53,000
Computer system analysts	41–43,000	47–49,000
Natural scientists	33–35,000	45–47,000
Physicians	—	55–59,000
Registered nurses	35–37,000	36–38,000
Therapists, occupations, physical, etc.	32–33,000	33–35,000
Teachers, college and university	—	43–45,000
Teachers, prekindergarten and kindergarten	22–24,000	29–31,000
Teachers, elementary school	27–30,000	32–34,000
Teachers, secondary school	28–30,000	34–36,000
Social workers	23–25,000	28–30,000
Lawyers	—	61–63,000
Designers	30–32,000	—

Technicians		
Health technologists and technicians	30–32,000	—
Computer programmers	36–38,000	45–47,000
Paralegals	32–34,000	—
Sales occupations		
Supervisors and proprietors	$32–34,000	$40–42,000
Insurance sales occupations	33–35,000	—
Real estate sales occupations	35–37,000	—
Sales representatives, mining, manufacturing, and wholesale	39–41,000	44–46,000
Sales workers, retail and personal services	19–21,000	22–24,000
Administrative support occupations, including clerical		
Supervisors	$30–32,000	—
Computer operators	23–25,000	—
Secretaries	20–22,000	—
Bookkeepers, accounting, and auditing clerks	21–23,000	—
Adjusters and investigators	25–27,000	—
Service occupations		
Police and detectives, except supervisors	$33–35,000	—
Food preparation and service occupations	15–17,000	—

Estimated Starting Salaries for 1994 Graduates with Bachelor's Degrees*

Bachelor's Degree	Salary Range
Chemical Engineering	$34–35,000
Computer Science	34–35,000
Mechanical Engineering	33–34,000
Electrical Engineering	33–34,000
Nursing	31–33,000
Physics	30–32,000
Civil Engineering	30–31,000

Accounting	29–30,000
Chemistry	28–29,000
Mathematics	27–28,000
Geology	26–27,000
Business Administration	24–25,000
Social Sciences	23–24,000
Liberal Arts	22–23,000

*Based on information from the U.S. Department of Labor

The Right Job Skills

Having the right skills, training, and education will be critically important in getting the right job. We have already seen from the information above that compensation will be impacted greatly by areas of study and occupation. It is no secret that earnings generally rise with education, and that the earnings of college graduates are significantly higher than workers with less education. Data from the Bureau of Labor Statistics show that during the 1980s and 1990s the relative earnings of college graduates also grew more rapidly than high school graduates and other non-college graduates.

In 1994 the average high school graduate is expected to earn about $13,000 per year compared to about $25,000 for the average college graduate with a bachelor's degree—representing over a ninety percent earnings premium for college graduates. Those with post-secondary vocational school and some college (but no degree) will earn about twenty percent more than high school graduates. The average worker with an associate degree can expect to receive about $20,000 per year or about fifty percent above high school graduates. Advanced college degree holders, such as master's, doctorate, and professional degrees, will have average annual compensation of about $33,000; $50,000; and $55,000 respectively.

There are many reasons why earnings increase with education. Firstly, many high-paid occupations are open only to people with certain credentials. For instance, a professional degree is needed to practice medicine, law, or dentistry. A bachelor's degree is usually required to enter many other well-paying occupations, such as accounting, computer science, engineering, teaching, and middle and senior-level management. Additionally, college graduates are typically more flexible and adaptable to new technologies and work assignments. They may have acquired specific skills in college—writing abilities, presentation skills, analytical and problem-solving skills—which are transferable across a diverse array of occupations. College graduates are more likely to take advantage of educational assistance programs, employer-sponsored training, and other forms of continuing education. They are also typically in a better position to promote themselves through community involvement, associations, and other forms of networking.

Some common job skills are: leadership and persuasion, helping and instructing others, creativity and problem-solving, initiative, teamwork, and public contact. Various occupations require some or all of these skills. People must continually review their skills to ensure that they match up with occupational and career objectives.

Leadership and persuasion skills involve the ability to manage people or to stimulate others to act in a certain way. These skills include organizing people, supervising, directing, promoting, counseling, and negotiating. They are required in a variety of occupations, such as executives, administrators, managers, urban planners, lawyers, teachers, professors, counselors, health practitioners, public relations specialists, editors, and marketing and sales representatives.

Helping/instructing skills include assisting, teaching, and counseling. These skills are used to help other people learn how to do or understand something. Instructing skills are not only required for teachers, college faculty, and counselors, but are also needed for executives, managers, computer systems analysts, lawyers, psychologists, physicians and health practitioners, health technicians, and sales and marketing personnel.

Problem-solving and creativity skills include designing, inventing, writing, and developing new ideas, programs or products. These skills are required in practically every occupation, with the exception of, perhaps, clerical administrative support and food service.

Initiative involves figuring out what needs to be done and completing the task without close supervision. This is also a characteristic that is beneficial to success in practically every occupation. Remember, successful people normally do not sit and wait for things to happen; rather, they make things happen.

The ability to work effectively as part of a team is becoming more and more important in today's business world of project teams, participative management, and other forms of group decision-making. Teamwork will inherently require good communication and people-oriented skills. The same applies to the ability to deal with the public on a regular basis.

CHAPTER THREE

FINDING AND KEEPING THE RIGHT JOB

*F*inding and keeping the right job is an important process for attaining career success. This process involves evaluating our interests and skills, matching them with job opportunities, and marketing our talents to prospective employers. Finding career and job information will involve networking with personal, business, and professional contacts. Resumés and interviews are essential in showing a person's background and experience and should be used effectively. Maintaining a good image and being an active participant will also be helpful to career advancement and fulfillment.

Marketing Our Talents

Each of us has talents and skills that we can sell. At the same time, there are many firms looking for skilled and talented people. Organizations need people to function. Even in the high-tech world of today and tomorrow, human resources are necessary to manage and service this high technology.

How do people obtain the job that they want? They do it by marketing their talents effectively. They must show prospective employers that they have the background and skills that these employers need.

The process of searching for the right job involves analysis, planning, and taking action. We should evaluate our interests and skills and match them up with job opportunities. Learn where to find job opportunities and how to apply for them. Prepare resumés, job applications, and cover letters for the best impact and effect. Prepare for job interviews by learning as much as possible about the prospective employer, anticipating issues and questions, and preparing a set of questions and concerns. Follow up after the interview. Even if a person doesn't get a particular job, he should use the job search and interview as a learning experience.

We should determine our job skills by making a list of our backgrounds and experiences. This should include education, specialized training, work experience, and volunteer activities. This list will be useful in filling out job applications, preparing resumés, and providing information on job interviews. Include in this list community activities, offices held in professional associations, part-time businesses, and hobbies. Think about the things done in everyday life, and the skills or talents it takes to do them. These skills can be useful in a job search to show a person's abilities.

Review interests and aptitudes. What are the things that are the most interesting. We should look at the list of our skills and talents and determine those which we like doing. What classes or training were liked? Why were they liked?

We need to determine what our career goals are. What kind of work do we want to be doing five or ten years from now? What kind of jobs can we get to help us reach these goals? All of these questions are important in helping us match our background and interests to job and career options, and in marketing our talents effectively.

Finding Career and Job Information

Good sources of career and job information are personal and business contacts, professional associations, educational institutions, personnel departments, recruiting and placement agencies, state employment service offices, public libraries, and others. Many of these sources are listed in the *Occupational Outlook Handbook* and in the appendix to this book. Also consult directories in the library's reference section for the names of potential sources. Start with *The Guide to American Directories, The Directory of Directories*, or *The Encyclopedia of Associations*—an annual multi-volume publication listing trade associations, professional organizations, and other groups. State employment service agencies develop detailed information about local labor markets, such as current and projected employment, characteristics of the work force, and changes in state and local economic activity.

Utilize all formal and informal job search methods. Review classified ads in newspapers, professional journals, and trade magazines. Realize that many job openings are not listed in the "Help Wanted" ads, and these ads may not offer much information about job descriptions, working conditions, or pay. Some may not even identify the employer, but merely give a post office box for sending your resumé. Never rely solely on classifieds to find a job. Respond to classifieds promptly, since jobs may be filled quickly, and keep a record of the ads to which a response was made.

A person can typically apply directly to prospective employers through their personnel or human resources offices. In fact, this is the most commonly-used job search method, and it has the highest effectiveness rate. A person should apply even if he does not know that an opening exists. It can be extremely helpful to a job applicant if someone refers him and there is a specific person he can contact.

The State Employment Service (typically called the "Job Service") operates about 1,700 local offices nationwide in coordination with the U.S. Employment Service of the Department of Labor. These offices provide help at no costs to jobseekers in locating employment. They provide job matching and referral services; a computerized daily job bank listing of public- and private-sector job openings; testing for occupational aptitude and interests and career counseling; and assistance in arranging interviews. Check the government telephone listings to locate the nearest office.

Private employment and recruiting agencies can be very helpful in a job search. These agencies can help save time and contact employers who otherwise might be hard to reach. Most operate on a commission basis and the applicant or the employer will have to pay this fee. Discuss the fees up-front and find out who is responsible for paying them. Try to deal with reputable recruiting agencies who will earn their fee from the employer, and who will respect any confidentiality in the job search.

College placement offices are another excellent resource for finding job openings and interviewing recruiters from prospective employers. Many college placement offices also offer career counseling, testing, workshops, videotapes, library services, reference materials, and career fairs to jobseekers. Also use the college placement offices as a means to network with alumni and faculty.

A large number of communities have career development, training, counseling, job placement, and employment services. These programs are sponsored by a variety of organizations, such as community agencies, churches and synagogues, and social service agencies. Use all of these to the maximum advantage.

Listed below are the most commonly-used job-search methods and their effectiveness-rates based on information from the U.S. Department of Labor.

Method	Percent Used	Effectiveness Rate
Applied directly to employer	66.0	47.7
Asked friends about their employers	50.8	22.1
Local newspaper ad	45.9	23.9
Asked friends about other employers	41.8	11.9
Asked relatives about their employers	28.4	19.3
Asked relatives about other employers	27.3	7.4
Private employment agency	21.0	24.2

Civil Service test	15.3	12.5
School placement office	12.5	21.4
Instructor or Professor	10.4	12.1

Another growing source of job and career information is Internet, a worldwide computer network of databases, computer services, and users. With the developing information superhighway, we can use a variety of online computer services, such as Compuserve, Prodigy, America Online, and Delphi, to access job listings, contact prospective employers, and network with other users for job leads, career prospects, and business opportunities.

The oldest and most comprehensive online service is Compuserve (phone: 800-848-8199), which provides a map to help users access the multitude of resources available. Prodigy is a mid-level online service (phone: 800-776-3449) best known for its graphics and bulletin boards. Newer online services such as America Online (phone: 800-827-6364) and Delphi (phone: 800-695-4005) generally provide a full range of Internet services at relatively cheaper rates.

All of these online services are accessible through personal computers, and they can connect us with millions of people at universities, libraries, companies, financial institutions, and government agencies. We can connect to worldwide files and databases, bulletin boards, professional associations, and other groups of special interest. We can contact these online services by calling their toll-free telephone numbers or obtaining starter kits and other information at computer shops and bookstores.

Creating an Effective Resumé

Employers want to hire people who have the background and skills to do the job. A resumé can be a highly effective way to present a person's talents and experience to potential employers. A resumé is normally required for professional, technical, administrative, managerial, sales, secretarial, clerical, and other office jobs.

A person needs information about himself and about the job he is seeking to prepare an effective resumé. Information about oneself includes skills, talents, work history, education, honors, community activities, professional organizations, hobbies, and other qualifications. Most of this information may have been prepared earlier as part of skills assessment and career planning. One should obtain specific information on the job he is applying for, such as education and experience requirements, salary range, job duties, work hours, location, and travel. He will need to know the new job responsibilities so that he can describe his experience in terms of those duties. Knowing the compensation on the new job will allow him to determine his own salary requirements, and to do a financial comparison if he is changing jobs. Use the information gathered to tailor a resumé to the specific job or career area being sought. A person may have to prepare several resumés if he is looking for different types of jobs.

The following information and format are usually included on every resumé:

- Name
- Address
- Telephone number
- Education, including school name and address, dates of attendance, areas of study, degrees awarded, and special honors and awards.
- Job experience, including job titles, names and addresses of employers, dates of employment, and job duties.
- Special skills, foreign languages, membership in organizations, and special awards.
- References, one should generally indicate that references will be available upon request. However, if the person reading the resumé is likely to know these references, then it may be worth listing the names on the resumé. Otherwise, keep handy the names, titles, addresses, and telephone numbers of three references.

There are two basic types of resumés for describing a

person's experience and employment history, the chronological resumé and the functional resumé. Good examples of a chronological and a functional resumé for a hypothetical college senior are reprinted in the Appendix from the *Occupational Outlook Quarterly*, Spring 1987. The type of format that should be used depends on where a person is in his career and how his progress has prepared him for the new job.

The chronological resumé is usually done in reverse chronology where someone describes his most recent job first and proceed backwards. He should use the chronological resumé if he has an established career path in a clearly defined area and want to move up to the next level. It may not be the best format if he is just entering the workforce, has very little work experience, has gaps in his employment history, or if the new job is very different from his current one.

A functional resumé emphasizes one's skills and abilities. Rather than a chronology of jobs, it gives a listing of skills and experience and the various jobs relating to these. A person prepares this resumé by first listing under his experience the information which most relates to the job he is seeking. This format allows the employer to immediately see how his abilities meet the job requirements. A functional resumé also de-emphasizes gaps in employment and less important jobs because it lists the most important jobs first and does not have to follow a time sequence.

Regardless of the format, a resumé should be accurate and specific. Be specific in identifying duties and accomplishments. One should use positive words which will emphasize his various skills. To highlight management skills use words like: administered, analyzed, coordinated, developed, directed, evaluated, improved, managed, organized, or supervised. To emphasize technical skills use words like: assembled, built, calculated, designed, operated, overhauled, remodeled, or repaired. Creative skills can be highlighted with words like: created, designed, established, fashioned, illustrated, invented, or performed. Show financial and marketing skills with words such as: administered, analyzed, balanced, budgeted, forecast, launched, marketed, planned, projected, sold, structured. Communication and instructional skills can be shown with: arranged, assessed, addressed, authored, counseled, facilitated, formulated, persuaded, represented, summarized, and the like. All of these words add action to a resumé.

Do not include negative or embarrassing information on a resumé. However, be prepared to deal with these situations positively at an interview or if questions otherwise come up. In general, do not include personal information, such as height, weight, physical condition, or marital status, unless it is specifically job-related. Additionally, do not put salary and wage information in a resumé.

A resumé should be concise and look professional. Proofread it carefully—it is a reflection of the job applicant. Have someone else review it for mistakes and clarity. Resumés should be typed, preferably printed, on 8½-by-11 inch quality white bond paper. A one-page resumé is best, and it should never exceed two pages.

Many large employers require jobseekers to complete an employment application form. If necessary, an applicant should use his resume to fit himself to a form. He should submit his resumé to accent his qualifications even if an employment application form is required. No matter how rigid the application form may appear, a person can still use it to focus on his strengths.

Submitting a powerful cover letter along with a resumé or application is always a smart maneuver in a job search. The cover letter should be succinct, yet interesting enough to capture the attention of the person receiving it. Show enthusiasm! Applicants should show that they have done some homework on the employer and understand its business and problems. They should use the cover letter to proclaim how their experience will benefit the employer and why they should be considered. Applicants should always indicate that they would welcome the opportunity to interview for the position.

Being Successful at Job Interviews

Job interviews are an important part of the job search process. In fact, most hiring decisions are made as a result of the first interview. Interviews are the best chance a person has to show a potential employer his qualifications and personal traits. Job interviews are an opportunity for him to shine. How someone is perceived at the interview could be more important than his actual experience and skills.

There are certain steps everyone should take to prepare for every job interview. He should learn as much as he can about the employer and the specific job for which he is interviewing. Review the qualifications for the job and have an updated resumé available. Think of answers to commonly-asked interview questions. Practice an interview with family or friends.

Some questions frequently asked of applicants during job interviews are:

- Why are you interested in this company or job?
- How did you find out about this job or company?
- Why should you be hired for the job?
- How would you describe yourself?
- How would other people describe you?
- Why did you choose this career?
- How is your background relevant to this job?
- What type of work do you like most?
- What are your major strengths?
- What are your biggest accomplishments?
- What are your major weaknesses?
- What things would you change in your life?
- What are your interests outside of work?
- What courses did you like the most or least in school?
- Why did you leave your last job?
- What did you like the most or least about your last job?
- What salary are you expecting?
- What do you see yourself doing five or ten years from now?
- What are your goals?

The best maneuver in responding to interview questions is to always focus on the job and one's skills. If asked about a strength or major accomplishment, mention something that relates to the new job. If asked about a weakness or negative factor from the past, turn it around positively. As a weakness, working too hard, being too concerned with details, wanting everything done right the first time, or demanding too much from oneself and others are good examples. If a negative issue arises, a person should emphasize that he learned from the situation and has overcome any shortcomings.

Jobseekers must recognize that a job interview is a two-way process. It is an opportunity for them to learn more about the employer, the job, and the people with whom they might be working. They should think about questions they want to ask the people interviewing them. What would a typical day on the job be like? What are the biggest challenges on the job? To whom would they report? Would they supervise anyone? What does the organization chart look like? What training is available? What are the opportunities for advancement? How important is the job? Why did the previous person leave the job? How is the company doing financially?

Questions about salary and benefits are usually held until the end of the interview. The primary focus at the interview should be the company, the new job, and how the applicant's abilities will benefit them. After the applicant has been offered the job, he can always negotiate the salary. He should be flexible in his salary requirements, but not sell himself short. Use the employer's quoted salary or salary range as the bottom point in salary negotiation, and explain why a higher salary is required to make the offer financially attractive. If a person is changing jobs he should typically seek a fifteen to twenty percent premium over his current salary, unless the new job offers other important benefits, such as greater advancement, supervisory experience, or better work environment.

The job interview is a chance for a person to show his best

side, including his personality and personal appearance. Dress professionally for job interviews, but dress to make an impact. It helps to know something about the organizational culture of the employer. Is it traditional? Conservative? Progressive? New wave? Each job candidate should try to show that he would make a good personal fit with coworkers and the organization's image. Maintain a well-mannered, yet confident demeanor. Use a firm handshake with men and women alike. Answer questions in a clear, concise, and positive manner. An applicant should always speak positively of former employers and coworkers, regardless of the circumstances under which he or she left.

Express interest in the job and the company, but let the interviewer direct the conversation. Candidates should ask questions during the interview process about things that they want to know. They should relax and be cooperative and enthusiastic. The interview should end on a positive note with the applicant reaffirming his interest in the job, and emphasizing that his background makes him a good candidate to fill the position.

Find out what the next step will be after the interview—will more interviews be necessary, will any additional information be required, and when will a final decision be made? The applicant should thank the employer for the interview and follow up promptly with a letter expressing his continued interest. A telegram or mail-gram is a quick and effective way to send a follow-up letter.

Every interview should be a learning experience. Even if a candidate is not actively looking for a job, he may want to go on a job interview once a year to explore opportunities, see how other shops operate, and keep his interviewing skills current. After each interview he should make a list of what went well and what things he can improve.

Being a Participant

To attain professional and personal fulfillment, a person cannot simply sit on the sidelines and watch things happen.

Rather, he must be an active participant in his work and community environment. Too often, people would rather complain about their situation than do anything about it. No one will be more effective in making things happen in a person's life than that person himself.

Participation is one of the most important factors contributing to quality of life. Participation can take many forms. On the job, for example, employee problem solving groups or quality circles are generally effective in addressing issues such as efficiency, productivity, communication, and getting people involved in making decisions which impact on their work and careers. Employee participation in profit-sharing has also been particularly effective in influencing performance, motivation, and commitment. Additionally, employee participation in the ownership of a company, such as stock ownership and voting rights, has demonstrated better sales growth and profit margins than conventional investor-owned enterprises.

Worker participation that is tied directly to financial incentives certainly tends to show increases in productivity, motivation, and overall job satisfaction. Participative strategies that change the work environment tend to have a lasting impact on attitudes and performance, especially if the changes involve increased responsibility and autonomy. Unfortunately, many organizations embody a structure, management style, and hierarchy which discourages people from taking initiative, accepting responsibility, and co-operating with coworkers. Our challenge is to change this norm, or to work within it with a participative approach which fosters input and involvement from everyone.

A large number of companies do encourage people to get involved in community, professional, and political activities. Having employees volunteer their time for good causes can have great public relations value to a firm. In fact, some companies consider community involvement as part of their performance appraisals and compensation reviews. In many positions, such as sales, marketing, and professional services, it can be a crucial networking tool. Work in community and professional associations can also offer a chance to develop managerial and leadership skills that a person might not obtain on his job. As a young professional, becoming a leader in a community project or professional organization may be the only opportunity to get to supervise people before turning thirty.

Participation in professional associations can lead to important contacts both inside and outside the firm. It can present unique opportunities to meet and have real-life talks with high level executives. A person can obtain timely and advantageous information about job openings and other career opportunities.

In the corporate downsizing and cost consciousness of the 1990s, some companies may not look favorably on outside activities. In these situations people must budget their time and choose their activities so that they have minimum effect on work responsibilities. People should find out if their firms support volunteerism, community involvement, and outside activities. Is the support real or merely superficial? Does the supervisor perceive this as valuable? Be sure to discuss any significant outside activities with the supervisor and personnel manager; emphasize the benefits. Try to choose community activities which are related to the company's business. Consider avoiding controversial issues such as abortion, gun control, or others which may not benefit the firm.

Keeping a Good Image

Our chances of keeping a good job and finding career success will depend a lot on our image and personality. Most of our image is comprised of what people perceive of us. So many things affect our image: our dress, our smile, how we talk, our sense of humor. We should make sure that we always project our best image.

Become a person other people respect and like being around. We have all seen people like this. They walk into a room and other people gravitate toward them. They have magnetic personalities, wit, and good conversation. They're smart.

We should look at ourselves and see how we can polish up

our images. We need to reach out to people by being friendly and courteous. Smile and speak to people. Be knowledgeable about current events and what's happening in our professions and at our firms. We should read the *Wall Street Journal*, *Business Week*, and the like, and at least two trade journals in our respective professions. A good conversationalist can speak on a variety of subjects. On the other hand, one shouldn't be a know-it-all whom people may consider obnoxious. We do not want to repel people with our smarts, but attract them.

Lighten up and relax around other people. People don't have to always be so serious. Quite often our fear of appearing foolish makes us uptight and uncommunicative. Laugh and keep a good sense of humor. Be attentive and listen to others. People like to feel that we have a real interest in what they have to say.

When entering a room, enter with a sense of confidence and maintain strong eye contact. If a person is late for a meeting, or has to present unpopular information, he or she should not enter with a defeated attitude. Rather, they should take a deep breath, gain their composure, and enter with an attitude of contribution.

A professional presence shows competence and credibility in business. How you dress determines a big part of your professional presence. Although standard business dress for men and women has not changed drastically over the past thirty years, a new dimension of *business casual* has been added to how we dress. The best formal business style for men is still the dark two-piece suit, preferably in navy, gray, charcoal, and black. However, the colors of tan, brown, dark green and medium blue are now also acceptable and friendly. Suits which are one hundred percent wool or a predominantly wool blend have the best appearance and wearability. A solid white, long-sleeve shirt remains the most appropriate choice, although light colors in blue, gray, beige, and pink are now considered stylish in many cases. Dress shirts should be one hundred percent cotton, or a blend which is primarily cotton, for the best look and comfort.

A necktie is perhaps the only means to add personality and uniqueness to a man's formal business dress. The colors of red, navy, and burgundy, in stripes or geometric shapes, continue to be the most popular. But, paisley and colorful patterns are a modern and stylish alternative. Ties preferably should be one hundred percent silk and should hang to about the middle of the belt buckle.

A man's shoes should fit comfortably and be well-maintained. Choose lace-ups, wingtips or slip-ons in black, dark brown, or burgundy leather. Jewelry should be kept to a minimum—a good quality watch and no more than one ring on each hand. Keep your hair neatly trimmed and your face cleanly shaven for the best professional look.

More and more companies are adopting business casual dress policies for Fridays, summer months, and many off-site meetings. Business casual provides the opportunity for some flexibility in a more relaxed, yet business-acceptable, dress. Business casual dress for men is usually slacks and a long or short-sleeve shirt or sweater. Jeans, under shirts and sweats are usually not appropriate for business casual. A tie and jacket should also be handy on business casual occasions in case the need arises for more formal dress.

The most popular professional style for a woman continues to be the business suit with matching skirt and jacket in navy, black, gray, and taupe. Other colors such as red, brown, blue, teal, and off-white are attractive and fashionable. The one- or two-piece dress is a more comfortable and informal business style. Business casual dress for women can be difficult to define, but a pants suit and long shorts, or skirt with a blouse or sweater are generally acceptable. Choose suits and dresses which are one hundred percent wool, silk, or predominant blends thereof. Blouses should be silk or cotton, and the colors of white, pink, blue, turquoise, emerald, and fuschia are recommended.

A woman's professional image continues with accessories such as jewelry, shoes, and makeup. Gold jewelry, such as a ring, watch, or earrings always accents a good business look, provided it is not overdone. Likewise, makeup which is applied subtly can enhance a woman's professional appearance. Black, navy, cream, and taupe leather shoes, especially leather pumps, are the best choices for women's shoes.

A strong sense of ethics is also extremely important for a successful professional image. Maintain high values, integrity, and a sense of fairness on and off the job. Don't be afraid to let clients, associates, or supervisors know if a proposed course of action is improper. Try to suggest reasonable and honorable alternatives to accomplish the desired objective. Avoid involvement in scandals, frauds, misrepresentations, and other unethical business and personal activities. Sometimes, just being near a scandal can taint a person's professional image and disqualify him from new opportunities. The key to determining the right or wrong course of action is to follow one's own conscience. If it's good enough for one as an individual, it should also be good enough for one's company.

CHAPTER FOUR

DEALING WITH JOB TRANSITIONS

*T*ransition is an inevitable part of work and family life. Whether we are starting a new job, getting a promotion, transferring to a new location, or going through periods of unemployment, transitions will provide us with opportunities, challenges, and stresses. Our success will depend largely on how we prepare for and manage these transitions in our lives.

There is no magic formula for effectively dealing with all the changes and transitions we will encounter in life. A good strategy is to always be flexible and prepare for anticipated transitions. Take the steps of analyzing the transition's effects, identifying potential problems and solutions, and taking appropriate action.

Life as a Business Cycle

A well recognized principle of economic theory is the business cycle. The business cycle is an attempt to explain the ups and downs of business performance, the "bull" to "bear" stock market activity, and the rise and fall in interest rates. There have been numerous theories advanced to explain the ups and downs of the economy that plague the performance of Wall Street's best. However, none of these theories are able to predict when an economic down- or up-turn is about to occur. At best, most economic theories are a history lesson—explaining what everyone already knows—it happened, and here is a possible explanation of what could have been the cause.

For whatever reason, business cycles happen. Time after time, prosperity and employment give way to economic recession and lay-offs. We cannot live in a capitalistic system of free enterprise and be free of these roller-coaster type changes as the economy moves from boom to bust, and as it passes from one stage of activity to another. The question is, what can each of us as an individual worker who sells our labor in the free enterprise system do to survive during periods of economic change?

We will all experience these personal business cycles and we must learn to apply our business and management skills to handling our own economic well-being. Our economic well-being will depend on our ability to recognize and handle personal highs and lows.

The first key to managing our personal business cycles is to recognize the change. How many people who are unemployed at this moment can say that it happened to them without any notice? They would have had to have been sleep-walking to have not recognized that something drastic was occurring in their jobs and the industry employing their services. Signs were everywhere that something adverse to their economic well-being was happening around them.

A period of transition can provide us with an opportunity to take or retake charge of our lives. It is a time for exploiting our uniqueness and not allowing circumstances to frustrate us. It is a time for reevaluating career and personal choices. Opportunities exist for those individuals who are willing to accept the challenges posed by these changes and to position themselves to be beneficiaries instead of victims of change.

Many of us have trained ourselves not to show fear. We hide it, bury it, do everything we can to conceal it. But fear is a normal human emotion. Think of our childhood—we were afraid of the dark, afraid of going to school, afraid to be separated from our families, afraid to go to camp for a week, afraid of the unknown. Each of us has fears, but we most often treat them as enemies, and try desperately to get rid of them, though we rarely succeed.

It is not always advantageous to get rid of fear. Fear can help us live and grow during times of transition. It calls our attention to essential things that need to be done. It causes us to analyze and plan for tough situations. We can either become wrapped-up in and destroyed by fear, or we can use it to our benefit. We can all find opportunities in fear to be creative and plan ahead.

Becoming Oriented to a New Job

Starting a new job can be a difficult transition. Most new employees face a kind of culture shock. Success in a new job will depend upon, among other things, an effective orientation to the new position and environment. An effective orientation program can help lessen the impact of this shock.

Our experiences during our first one or two years on a new job can have a big impact on our careers with those organizations. We will need to learn our job expectations and how to quickly become contributing members of our organization. To be oriented to a new job, a person will need specific information on his company's standards, traditions, policies, social behavior, and work climate, as well as the technical aspects of the job.

Although nearly seventy percent of employers provide some form of orientation to new employees, in many cases this is merely a superficial indoctrination into company policies and rules. Often this amounts to nothing more than a presentation of an employee handbook and a quick tour of the office. The new employee is then immediately put to work in a sink-or-swim environment. Clearly, employers need to do a better job in planning, implementing, and evaluating their orientation programs. However, the new employee should find out the elements of an effective orientation and take the necessary steps to make this happen.

An ideal orientation would provide the new employee with current department and company organization charts; copies of any policy handbooks; a copy of the specific job description; list of training opportunities; information on career paths and advancement; an overview of company products, services, and customers; information on financial performance, growth, and trends; locations and telephone numbers of key people and operations; copies of important company publications; performance evaluation forms and procedures; lists of employee benefits; and a mentor to promote and counsel the new employee.

Because all of these materials are not normally supplied, we will have to learn about our organizations from a variety of sources. These include official company literature, policies set by upper management, instructions from supervisors, examples from peers, performance evaluations and feedback, informal discussions and socialization with coworkers. Organizations generally are better at communicating factual information about compensation, benefits, and company policies than about company attitudes, acceptable norms of behavior, and what it takes to be successful. The onus is primarily on each of us to maximize our orientation to a new job.

Don't become a victim of poor orientation and socialization in a new job. Be sure to seek important assignments upfront, instead of insignificant duties and tasks which are frequently used to teach the job from the ground up. Successful people show that they are ready for the challenges of the new job and able to contribute to the organization from day one. At the same time, a new employee shouldn't become overwhelmed and suffocated by the mass of information which may be thrown at him. He should become part of the social and informal network in his organization. He should get involved in department- and company-sponsored social events—the company golf league, office parties, charitable functions and the like. This guided self-learning is important in preparing men and women alike for the social and cultural context of the new job, and is likely to be crucial to overall career success.

Handling Job Moves

Flexibility, adaptability, and mobility are key factors in career success. A professional worker is unlikely to spend his or her entire worklife with a single employer or in the same job or location. National and international companies often require workers to accept assignments thousands of miles away from home and the main office. Many organizations also request that employees accept a promotion or make lateral job transfers between departments for a variety of staffing, strategic, or developmental reasons.

A willingness to move on the job, functionally or geographically, can show loyalty to the firm and the desire to do what is best for the company. A job move can also provide opportunities for career growth, advancement, and autonomy which may not be available in the current job or at the main office. Some job moves, however, instead of boosting a person's career, can actually stall it.

There are four basic types of moves an individual can make in an organization: up, over, down, or out. These moves are frequently influenced by his decision to make a career advancement or change, or by internal staffing decisions of the organization. Each type of move involves special issues and concerns which require analysis and adaptability.

Upward moves or promotions are almost always felt as positive job moves. The person promoted normally assumes more important job responsibilities and higher compensation and benefits. Promotions are also less emotionally traumatic than the other job moves, unless, perhaps, if a major relocation is involved. There can, however, be stressful issues regarding coworkers; particularly those who may have been passed over for the same promotion or whom the promoted worker may now supervise or work with directly. These situations are likely to require special sensitivities on the part of the person promoted. He will need to reach out to peers he may have left behind, particularly if he is now their supervisor. He should make them a part of his decision-making process and find ways to mentor and promote them. The promoted worker is now in a leadership position, and his success will unequivocally depend upon the motivation and cooperation of the people reporting to him.

Downward job moves or demotions can be extremely

difficult situations. They typically result from disciplinary action, inability to manage in a higher-level job, illness, or workforce reductions. Although a move down may be preferable to being terminated in many situations, the demoted worker generally must prepare psychologically for a cut in pay and grade level. A depressed morale can lead to inefficiency and strained inter-actions with coworkers, unless he finds value in his continuing contribution or an alternative career path.

Career development has historically been seen in terms of moves up the corporate ladder, with lateral job moves typically viewed as stagnation or failure. The corporate downsizing of the 1980s and 1990s has resulted in flatter organizations and a rethinking of the value of horizontal job moves. Many companies are encouraging intraorganizational mobility as a means to keep valued employees motivated and challenged and to broaden their horizons.

Lateral job transfers must be analyzed to make sure that they offer real opportunity and are consistent with career goals. Will the move enhance one's standing within the organization? Will it offer greater experience, exposure, or visibility? Will it help develop skills that enhance marketability for the next big move?

A relocation can be another source of job opportunities and problems. For the relocating worker, it can mean a job promotion with increased pay and prestige. However, relocations can cause many complications for the spouse and family of the relocated employee, such as loss of friends and community ties, joblessness or job change for the spouse, and uprooting the kids from school. There are also major financial considerations in a relocation, with the total costs of relocating often exceeding $50,000.

Most major companies and firms have relocation assistance programs which pay for house-hunting trips, shipping and storage of household items, temporary living expenses at the new location, expenses of selling and buying a home, and mortgage interest and cost of living differentials. Many also provide equity loans and a bonus of one month's salary to cover various incidentals. Always review the company's program if a relocation is being considered so that its coverage is fully understood. Sometimes additional features can be negotiated which are not covered by the regular relocation package.

With many companies going through globalization, job transfers to foreign countries are highly likely. This can also result from the increasing number of Americans working for foreign-based companies. Although foreign assignments can be a real boost to a person's career, there can also be some unexpected pitfalls. People can get lost in the shuffle by being away from the home office and find it difficult to fit back in upon their return. Before taking a foreign assignment make sure that it is strategically important to the company and to one's career development. Try to get a written commitment that an equivalent or greater job will be available upon returning home. If not, have the company commit to a generous severance package if it can not offer an equal position. Maintain close ties to mentors at the main office to keep from losing touch with corporate culture and politics. Visit the home office as often as possible and otherwise keep in contact via telephone, fax, or electronic mail and the like.

Moving out of an organization can occur through resignations, retirements, layoffs, and dismissals. Each involves a special set of circumstances and concerns. If someone decides to resign to pursue other interests, he shouldn't burn any bridges, but try to leave on amicable terms. A counter-offer may be presented by the current employer if the departing employee is a valued one, but it is usually advantageous in the long-term to go forward with the decision to leave once it has been announced. In most cases the circumstances leading to the decision to move on will remain unchanged, and the employee's loyalty is always likely to be questioned if he stays on.

Preparing for Unemployment

Joseph Boyett and Henry Conn, in their book, *Workplace 2000*, (New York, Penguin Group, 1991, p.44) had this to say about the need for all Americans to prepare for periods of unemployment:

"With Workplace 2000, the days of job stability are at an end. No more will an American worker expect to join a company and stay with that company until retirement. Most Americans will experience repeated job changes throughout their careers and perhaps months of unemployment as they move from one failed ... company to a new business ..." Since every one of us can expect periods of unemployment, this underscores the need to prepare and plan for joblessness. Having six months or more of salary available in cash or other liquid assets will be critical to financial survival during unemployment.

How do we develop a financial strategy for the periods we may be jobless through the corporate downsizing of the 1990s? During this period, newly unemployed professionals and middle managers will be in their forties and fifties. They will spend most of their money on sending their children to college and helping their elderly parents, instead of saving. Although they have another ten to twenty working years left, finding a new job could take a year or more. Although people in their twenties and thirties might find it easier than their older colleagues to get new jobs, many of them will still have to cope with six months or more of unemployment.

A good financial game plan in case of unemployment should be to trim debt, particularly credit card and other high-interest debt; obtain maximum benefits from severance, unemployment compensation, and other entitlements; and minimize your tax liabilities. Cut down on nonessentials, but not to the extent that life can't be enjoyed, such as going out to dinner or a show sometimes. Because unemployment can be a period of depression and anxiety, people are likely to feel better about themselves if they can continue their basic lifestyles.

Apply for unemployment compensation as early as possible. Don't be ashamed to collect unemployment compensation—we are entitled to it. These funds can be extremely important in helping make ends meet until a new job is found.

Terminated employees should review their severance

package to make sure they are getting everything which is due them. Most companies give employees one week of severance pay for each year of service. This severance may, typically, be enhanced to provide incentives for some employees to leave voluntarily. Although most people take their severance as a lump sum, this may not be the best approach from a tax standpoint. A person may end up paying a higher tax rate on his regular salary when combined with a lump sum severance paid in the same year. It may be advantageous to have your severance paid over a year or more to benefit from the lower tax rates due to reduced earnings while unemployed. Also, people shouldn't rush out with their severance or other savings to buy a small business without evaluating the market.

Workers who are terminated should make certain that they or their ex-employer maintain their health insurance coverage. Many companies will continue to pay health insurance for a period of time for employees who are laid-off or take early retirement. Under federal law they have the option to continue their employer-sponsored group health insurance for eighteen months or more. The costs for continuing group health insurance will still be substantially less than if they had to obtain health insurance on their own.

Careful consideration should be given to how to handle the money in a 401(k) plan or other tax-deferred savings plans. Usually any distributions received from these plans before age 59½, must be rolled over to an individual retirement account or other tax-deferred plan within sixty days to avoid taxes and penalties.

Many times it is possible to negotiate a severance package. Even a voluntary severance can be negotiated where a company may be undergoing a staff reduction and want to minimize layoffs. On many occasions, professional employees have been successful in striking deals with their employers to perform part or all of their former job as independent contractors.

CHAPTER FIVE

PURSUING YOUR OWN BUSINESS

More and more people are looking at starting their own business instead of seeking traditional employment. Business ownership can provide many advantages such as independence, autonomy, motivation, and professional growth. But, it also requires commitment, business skills, financing, and many other resources. Whether buying an existing business or franchise, or starting a new one, a person should carefully analyze his or her skills, the business opportunities and the risks. Find out what are the best business prospects and how to access the resources needed to pursue them. What is the right product or service to put on the market? What is the best form of business organization? What laws, regulations, and record keeping requirements will apply? These are some of the many questions that will need to be answered before starting a business.

Going Into Business For Yourself

Starting a business may be an attractive alternative to seeking career success in corporate America. An outside business can even be beneficial on a part-time basis while a person continues in his regular job. It can broaden his background and experience, and it can provide additional sources of income and new career paths.

But entrepreneurship may not be for everyone. We may not

have the characteristics of a true entrepreneur. Further, we may not want to invest the time and resources that a successful business requires. To be sure about entrepreneurship, a person should study the characteristics of successful business owners to see if he has the right traits.

Involvement in one's business could in some cases conflict with a full-time position. If there is a potential for conflict, the outside business activities should be reviewed with supervisors. Emphasize how it supplements present job experiences, keeps skills current, and increases well-roundedness. Stress that it will not detract from work and performance. Where no conflict is likely between job and business endeavors, there is less of a need to make it an issue.

Studies have shown that entrepreneurs are generally people who have high initiative, are self-confident, set long-term goals, are able to solve problems, take appropriate risks, learn from mistakes, and use all available resources. They compete with themselves and believe that success or failure lies within their personal control and influence.

People must determine why they want to go into business. Are they unhappy with their present jobs? Is business ownership part of their career goals? Do they have skills which are useful in their businesses? Who can they go to for assistance?

The U.S. Small Business Administration offers many publications and other sources of assistance to small business owners. The following helpful pamphlets are available for a small fee by writing to Small Business Administration, P.O. Box 15436, Fort Worth, TX 76119:

Thinking About Going into Business	MA 2.025
Checklist For Going into Business	MA 2.016
Ideas into Dollars	SBB 91
Selecting the Legal Structure for Your Business	MA 6.004
Marketing for Small Business	SBB 89
Keeping Records in Small Business	MA 1.017

The following informative SBA publications are available from the Superintendent of Documents, U.S. Government Printing Office, Washington, D.C. 20402:

Starting and Managing a Small Business of Your Own— Starting and Managing Series No. 1; and *Starting and Managing a Business from Your Home*. The following excerpts from these publications are helpful in reviewing the decision to pursue a potential business endeavor.

Answering some basic questions upfront about their abilities and their business endeavors can provide reality testing for people's ideas. They can order a copy of the SBA pamphlet *Checklist for Going into Business*. Answer the questions and discuss their reactions with friends and family. Or better yet, they should ask several people close to them to think carefully about them and fill out the checklist for them. Have they underestimated their abilities? Overestimated them? Sometimes an evaluation by a friend is more useful than a self-evaluation.

A person pursuing his own business must think about what resources are available to him. Will he start by keeping his job and "moonlighting" for a while? Does he have a small nest egg, inheritance, or retirement income to live on until he gets the business going? Does he already own tools or machines that will help (for instance, a word processor for a secretarial business or professional cameras and a darkroom for a commercial photography business)? Is he able to go back to school for training if necessary? Has he built up a network of contacts and possible customers through his previous lines of work or will he be starting from scratch?

Answering these questions honestly and completely will help one assess not only the chances of success but also which type of business to choose. For instance, if one's past professional life and contacts are all in the educational, teaching, child-oriented school area, then he should be sure he has powerful reasons for leaving that area and opening a mail-order seed business. Possibly a tutoring business or a tot exercise franchise would use more of his resources and networks. On the other hand, if his assessment of his life goals and preferences helps him realize that he is burned out from working with kids, then perhaps a business planning birthday parties could later be built into a general party planning and catering business. He would then be using his old contacts to build a long-range business plan that focuses on a service business for adults.

Your Next Steps

What's the perfect part-time or full-time business to get into? We've listed our skills. We've outlined our interests. We've described our family's preferred lifestyle. We've come up with a business idea. Next, we should consider such questions as: Are there customers for my product or service? How do I know? How will I find them? Who are my competitors? What will I charge? How will I promote my product or service? Finding the answers to these questions is the challenging and sometimes tedious homework that will help us determine our chances for success, and whether we should look for another more-marketable idea. Keep in mind that a person may be able to start and operate a business, particularly a part-time one, out of his home.

Developing a professional image may be hard if we work out of our home. Projecting a businesslike image is an important part of building credibility with our customers and contributes to our own professional self-image. Design a logo or have one designed; order business cards and stationery. Set regular business hours. Use an answering machine or answering service. If other members of the family also answer the phone, make sure they know what to say. Have a businesslike office or "showroom" if meeting customers face to face. Consider referring to the apartment number as "suite number" or rent a post office box. Such practices might improve the chances of doing business with potential customers.

The first step in creating a business is for a person to decide what his or her product or service is. What is he selling? He should practice writing a short, specific statement describing the product or service. Getting a clear idea of a business concept is one of the most difficult tasks in creating a business. The statement may change several times as one experiments with the market and tests one's skills. Instead of "I make toys," he or she may want to narrow the product line to "I make wooden dolls." Instead of "I write software programs for small business needs," he or she may decide to tap into a big market and "provide training for employees of small businesses in the use of accounting packages." He should see how it feels to describe the product or service to family, friends, potential customers, and fellow business people. Is the description clear and brief? Can he say it with confidence and enthusiasm?

To develop and test the business idea, one should answer the question: "Who will buy my product or service?" One should make a list of potential customers: individuals, groups, segments of the population, or other businesses that need the product or service. If he or she is making fabric-covered lap boards for people confined to bed, how will they quickly and inexpensively find a market? Through hospitals or home nursing care organizations? Through craft stores by displaying them as gift items? In mail order catalogues? Is there a market avenue that will reach children? One should ask friends and colleagues for help in brainstorming all the possible customers, markets, and uses for his product or service.

One's business planning must also include an up-to-date analysis of the competition. Why? Because one needs to plan one's market position—how one will fit into the marketplace. Will the product or service be cheaper or more expensive than that of the major competitors? Will it be more durable? Will the business be open during hours that competitors are closed? What benefits can be built into the product or service that the competitors don't offer? Will you do rush jobs?

In planning one's business, you should look for a unique niche that will give freedom from strong competition or that will make the product or service more valuable than others in the market. If you plan to open a day-care center and finds that none in the area is open before school, early opening might make the service more competitive. If you discover that local caterers have overlooked the office party market, you might highlight that in your brochure. The more you can learn about the competition, the better you'll be able to decide how to position yourself in the market.

Newspaper ads and trade magazines are other good sources of market information. Check also with the Chamber of Commerce, the county office of economic development, the Census Bureau, and business and professional organizations to gather market and pricing data.

Where Are Your Customers?

As the new business owner becomes more familiar with the competition, he will also be discovering where and how to find customers. Whatever the type of business he wants to open, he will need to do market research to determine if there are buyers for his idea, where they are, and how to find them. And in the process, he will also be gathering information on pricing.

Visit the local library to compile local and county statistics on the size and makeup of the market. While at the library, check out some books on marketing research. Also, check the following resources that might have data about the product or service or the people who would use it:

- *Encyclopedia of Associations*, 17th Edition. Gale Research Company, Book Tower, Detroit, MI 48226.
- *Ayer Directory of Publications*. Lists trade publications by subject matter. Contact the sales, marketing, or research departments for buying patterns among their readers.
- "Survey of Buying Power." *Sales, Marketing, Management* Magazine. July issue each year.
- *Thomas' Register*. Lists companies by product and service line, organized geographically and alphabetically.

- *Directory of Business, Trade, and Public Policy Organizations.* U.S. Small Business Administration, Office of Advocacy.
- Department of Commerce Publications. Data User Series Division, Bureau of the Census, Washington, D.C. 20233.
- *County Business Patterns.* U.S. Department of Commerce, Bureau of the Census. Available for each state.

When the marketing research is completed it will have 1) identified potential customers; 2) helped discover their habits, needs, preferences, and buying cycles; and 3) provided insight on how to reach them to generate sales.

Promotion is an overall, long-range plan designed to inform potential customers about what is being sold. Advertising is usually thought of as the paid communication part of the promotion program.

To develop a total promotional campaign one must answer these questions: 1) What image or message do I want to promote? 2) What are the best media and activities for reaching my potential customers? 3) How much time and money can I spend on the effort?

One should develop a long-range, consistent program for building image and reaching customers. His image should be reflected in his business card, logo, stationery, brochure, newsletter, telephone answering service, signs, paid ads, and promotional activities.

Word-of-mouth recommendations from satisfied customers are the very best promotion any business can have. One should consider which promotional tactics will build the confidence and image he is looking for—giving speeches and interviews (often good for counselors, teachers, lawyers, consultants), having an open house or holiday home sale (for crafts people), holiday recitals or shows (for music and dance teachers or day-care operators), free demonstrations and samples (for retailers, decorators, caterers).

Several small ads may have more impact than one large,

splashy ad. Conduct a campaign rather than having a one-shot ad or event. If hiring a public relations firm, look for one that can give personal attention and develop a total marketing plan, not just a couple of ads. The plan should include market research, a profile of the target audience, a clear description of the image they want to project, the written copy, and a list of media (including cost and scheduling calendars) that are best for that type of product or service. Most new small business owners will probably want to set aside a certain dollar amount per year or a percentage of past, current, or projected sales for paid advertising.

Should You Buy an Existing Business?

Although it is fascinating starting something from ground zero, the problems associated with organizing a new business may be lessened if buying an existing business.

Some advantages of buying an existing business are:

- It takes much less time and effort to get the business to a break-even point. It is even possible to earn a profit from the beginning.
- An existing business already has a market and customer base.
- Equipment and merchandise are likely to already be in place.
- An existing business has employees familiar with the business.
- Less financial outlays may be required with an existing business than with starting a new one.
- If the existing business is somewhat successful, the risks of failure are lessened.

There could be some disadvantages to buying an existing business. A person could be buying the previous owner's headaches, problems, and mistakes. There may be internal problems that only the seller knows about. There are no guarantees the business will continue to be profitable after taking it over. A person may be misled into paying too much. The accounts receivable may be high and largely uncollectible. The owner's departure may have a negative effect on employees and customers.

Evaluating a business that a person is about to buy is a critical process. He should do his homework by speaking with other business people in the area, customers, suppliers, current and former employees, and trade associations. Ask for bank references and contact the Better Business Bureau to find out about any complaints. He should also visit the business and spend time observing the appearance, location, clients, management, and organization.

Here are some issues and information that should be evaluated before buying a business:

- Financial records: Get copies of the financial statements and tax returns. An audit will be needed that gives an accurate picture of the financial health of the company. Retain a certified public accountant to review and audit the records for correctness.
- Inventory: Have the inventory appraised. Observe its condition and saleability and determine its value.
- Buildings & Equipment: Take along an expert to look at buildings and equipment. What are they worth? Are modifications needed?
- Liabilities: Are there any unpaid bills, back taxes, or pending litigation? The purchasing contract should provide that any claims against the business before the purchaser take ownership are the sole responsibility of the seller.
- Personnel: A successful business will have key personnel who are responsible for its success. Will they remain after takeover of the business?
- Customers: Talk with customers and find out whether they will continue their support with the new owner.
- Suppliers: Will suppliers continue to accommodate the business? Are they reliable or are changes necessary?
- Seller cooperation: Will the seller help during the transition period? Try to determine the owner's real motivation

for selling the business. Have the seller sign a non-compete clause to prevent customers from following him or her after the sale.

Buying a Franchise

Franchising—the very word suggests success and big profits to many people. Franchising may be an attractive option for someone who wants to own a business. Franchises today account for more than a third of the total U.S. retail economy.

A person could consider franchising if he wants to own a business but does not want to start from the ground floor or undertake the effort and risk of developing a new product or service. He should also consider it if he wants to be self-employed, but has no expertise in any particular area or lack some of the skills necessary to start a business.

Franchising is a relationship in which the franchisee undertakes to conduct a business, or sell a product or service in accordance with the methods and procedures prescribed by the franchisor. The franchisor usually agrees to assist the franchisee through advertising, promotion, and other advisory services.

Here are some advantages to buying a franchise:
* The product or service has already been developed.
* The franchise often has name recognition.
* The franchisor assists in running the business.
* The franchisor can help in obtaining financing.
* A franchise can earn a profit sooner than a self-start business because the product or services have been field tested and are often established.
* Through the mass purchasing power of the franchisor, the franchisee can save on the costs of goods and supplies.
* Through the pooled advertising funds of the various franchisees, the business will benefit from advertising that an independent business most likely couldn't afford.

There are also several negatives about franchising that should be considered, such as:

* Although it is technically his business, the franchisee is legally bound to abide by certain guidelines established by the franchisor. Each franchisor's guidelines are different.
* Conflict between franchisor and franchisee can result because the franchisor usually wants a lot of control over what he has built up while the franchisee wants to be an independent businessperson. Some franchisors provide more freedom that others, which is why it is important that a person fully research the company he is interested in before buying.
* Keep in mind that the franchisee is buying a franchise license which allows him to use the franchise's name, products and services. For this he pays a lot of money to the franchisor.
* Franchise fees can cost anywhere from 350 to over a millon dollars depending on the company. Much of it must be paid up front. (See chart below on the fastest growing franchises in the U.S.)
* The franchisee is dependent on the success of the franchisor. Even if he develops a successful business, it is impossible to continue his operation if his franchisor goes out of business.
* The franchisor typically has the right to terminate the franchise if the franchise does not abide by the rules, or the franchisor may be able to buy back the franchise whenever it wants.
* Despite promising market research showing strong consumer demand, competition from similar businesses or changing consumer tastes could leave the franchisee vastly short of the projected amount of business.

The following list, based on information from *Entrepreneur* magazine, shows the fastest growing franchises in the United States in 1992, including the area of business and the typical start-up costs.

Franchise	Area of Business	Start-up cost
Subway	Sandwiches	$ 40,000
7-Eleven	Convenience stores	13,500
Jani-King	Commercial cleaning	1,500
Burger King	Fast food	275,000
Dunkin' Donuts	Donuts/Coffee	175,000
McDonald's	Fast food	Varies
Coverall N. America	Commercial cleaning	350
Cleannet	Commercial cleaning	0
Little Ceasar's Pizza	Pizza	170,000
Mail Boxes etc.	Packaging, mailing & shipping services	28,000
Chem-Dry	Carpet, upholstery, & drapery services	7,000
Domino's Pizza Inc.	Pizza	77,000
O.P.E.N. Cleaning Sys.	Commercial cleaning	500
Miracle Ear	Health-care equipment	35,000
Choice Hotels Int'l	Hotels and motels	1,500,000
Micro-Age Computer Centers	Computer supplies	56,000
Blockbuster Video	Video rentals	365,000
Jazzercise	Fitness centers	2,000
Worldwide Refining Systems	Porcelain/marble restoration	6,500
Travelodge	Hotels and motels	500,000
Merry Maids	Residential cleaning	7,500
Futurekids	Computer learning centers	20,000
GNC	Health food & vitamin stores	38,000
Play It Again Sports	Sports equipment/apparel	68,000
H & R Block	Income tax services	5,000
Howard Johnson	Hotels and motels	Varies
Decorating Den	Decorative products	9,000
Re/Max Int'l	Real estate services	50,000
Valet Park	Personal services	4,000
Super 8 Motels	Hotels and motels	150,000

Before entering into a franchise agreement, inquire about the franchisor at the Better Business Bureau, local bank, and Chamber of Commerce. Also, consider how many competing franchises already exist. Obtain preliminary information from the franchisor and review it before making any commitments. The Federal Trade Commission Franchise Rule requires all franchisors to disclose the names and addresses of franchisees closest in proximity to the prospective franchisee. Ask those franchisees their opinion of the franchisor, the problems they have incurred, how much they paid, what kind of profits they are making, if the franchisor is accessible to their needs, and any other information they are willing to share.

Choosing Your Form of Business Organization

One of the most important decisions a business owner will make is whether to set up the business as 1) a sole proprietorship; 2) a partnership; or 3) a corporation. Note however, that the small business owner essentially risks it all, no matter what form of business organization he chooses.

The forming of a business organization depends on a number of important factors such as:

- Legal restrictions
- Need for capital
- Liabilities assumed
- Number of people associated in the venture
- Kind of business or operation
- Tax advantages or disadvantages
- Intended division of earnings
- Perpetuation of the business

Although most small businesses are sole proprietorships or partnerships, the following comparison of the advantages and disadvantages of each type of organization should be made:

- A sole proprietorship is the least costly way of starting a business. A person can form a sole proprietorship by finding a location and opening the door for business.

89

There are the usual fees for registering the business name and for legal work in changing zoning restrictions and obtaining necessary licenses. Attorney's fees for starting a sole proprietorship will be less than for the other forms because less document preparation is required.

Here are some advantages and disadvantages of the sole proprietorship:

ADVANTAGES
* Easiest to get started
* Greatest freedom of action
* Maximum authority
* Income tax advantages in very small firms
* Social Security advantage to owner

DISADVANTAGES
* Unlimited liability
* Death or illness endanger business
* Growth limited to owner's energies
* Personal affairs easily mixed with business

* A partnership can be formed by simply making an oral agreement between two or more persons, but such informality is not recommended. Legal fees for drawing up a partnership agreement are higher than those for a sole proprietorship, but may be lower than incorporating. Partners would be wise, however, to consult an attorney to have a partnership agreement drawn up to help resolve future disputes.

Here are some advantages and disadvantages of the partnership form of business:

ADVANTAGES
* Two heads better than one
* Additional sources of venture capital

DISADVANTAGES
* Difficult to transfer interest
* Death, withdrawal, or bankruptcy of one partner endangers business

- Better credit rating than corporation of similar size

- Personal liability for Partnership obligations
- Difficult to get rid of bad partner
- Hazy line of authority

- A special form of business organization is the limited partnership, which combines features of a general partnership and a corporation. With this form there must always be at least one general partner who remains personally liable for partnership liabilities. The limited partners are usually only liable up to the extent of their investment in the limited partnership. This exemption from personal liability normally continues as long as the limited partner does not participate in the management or control of the business. As many complex issues may arise with a limited partnership, it is recommended that legal counsel be obtained.
- A corporation is the most complex of the business forms and statutory requirements must be met to bring it into existence. A corporation is a separate legal entity which is established pursuant to state law. As a separate legal entity, a corporation can contract in its own name, hold property in its own name, and can sue and be sued in court in its own name.

The formation of a corporation requires the preparation of Articles of Incorporation which are filed with the Secretary of State for the state where the corporation is being formed. The Articles of Incorporation usually include the name of the corporation, its location and registered agent, its purposes, the amount and classes of stocks, the first Board of Directors, and the names and addresses of the incorporators. Generally, once the Articles of Incorporation are filed and approved by the Secretary of State, the corporation comes into existence.

A business owner can incorporate without an attorney, but he may be unwise to do so. People may think a small family corporation does not need an attorney, but an attorney can save members of a family corporation from hard feelings and family squabbles. Attorney's fees may run high if organization problems are complex. The corporate form is usually the most costly to organize.

Here are some advantages and disadvantages of the corporate form of business:

ADVANTAGES	DISADVANTAGES
• Limited liability for stockholders (while true for big business, may not be for small business)	• Gives owner a false sense of security
• Continuity	• Heavier taxes
• Transfer of shares	• Power limited by Charter
• Easier to raise capital	• Less freedom of activity
• Possible to separate business functions into different corporations	• Legal formalities
	• More expensive to launch

A corporation is generally taxed as a separate entity and shareholders are also taxed on corporate income paid to them as dividends. However, the election of Subchapter S status allows an eligible corporation to escape the double taxation. The purpose of Subchapter S is to permit a "small business corporation" to elect to have its income taxed to the shareholders as if the corporation were a partnership. Subchapter S status, overcomes the double taxation of corporate income, and permits the shareholders to have the benefit of offsetting business losses by the corporation against the income of the shareholders.

Among the qualifying requirements of electing and maintaining Subchapter S eligibility are that the corporation be a U.S. corporation having no more than thirty-five shareholders, all of whom are individuals or estates; that there by no nonresident alien shareholders; that there be only one class of issued stock; and that all shareholders consent to the election. An election for

Subchapter S status requires that the corporation file Form 2553 with the Internal Revenue Service.

Recordkeeping

Keeping accurate and up-to-date business records is, for many people, the most difficult and uninteresting aspect of operating a small business. If this area of business management is one that the business owner anticipates will be hard for him, he shall plan now how he will cope with it. Don't wait until tax time or until things are totally confused. Take a course at the local community college, ask a volunteer SCORE® (Service Corps of Retired Executives) representative from the Small Business Administration to help in the beginning, or hire an accountant to give advice on setting up and maintaining a recordkeeping system.

Business records will be used to prepare tax returns, make business decisions, and apply for loans. Set aside a special time each day to update business records. It will pay off in the long run with more deductions and fewer headaches.

If the business is small or related to an activity that is usually considered a hobby, it's even more important that good records be kept. The IRS may decide that the activity is only a hobby, and deductions for expenses or losses from home-produced income won't be allowed at tax time. So a business owner should keep records of all transactions in which he spends or brings in money.

Pick a name for the business and register it with local or state regulatory authorities. Call city hall or the county courthouse to find out how.

The business records should ideally tell how much cash is owed, how much cash is due, and how much cash is on hand. A business owner should keep these basic records:

- Check Register—Shows each check disbursed, the date of disbursement, number of the check, to whom it was made out (payee), the amount of money disbursed, and for what purpose.

- Cash Receipts—Shows the amount of money received, from whom, and for what.
- Sales Journal—Shows the business transaction, date, for whom it was performed, the amount of the invoice, and the sales tax, if applicable. It may be divided to indicate labor and goods.
- Voucher Register—A record of bills, money owed, the date of the bill, to whom it is owed, the amount, and the service.
- General Journal—A means of adjusting some entries in the other four journals.

Business records should be set up to reflect the amount and type of activity in the particular business. There are a wide range of pre-packaged recordkeeping systems. The SBA's pamphlet *Small Business Bibliography*, No. 15 lists many such systems. The most useful system for a small business is usually based on what is called the "One-Write System." It captures information at the time the transaction takes place. These One-Write Systems are efficient because they eliminate the need for recopying the data and are compatible with electronic data processing if the business owner should decide to computerize.

Even though the business may be small and just beginning, it is probably wise to consult an accountant to help decide which recordkeeping system is best for the business. Once it is set up, the owner can record the daily transactions in his general ledger and prepare his financial statements.

Be sure to establish a separate bank account for the business—even before the first sale. Then the owner will have a complete and distinct record of his income and expenditures for tax purposes, and he won't have to remember which expenses were business and which were personal.

It is important to choose a recordkeeping system that will be understood and will be used. It will help the business owner see how well the business is doing and is the first step in responsible financial management.

Working with Professionals

Even the smallest and newest business needs help from at least two kinds of specialists: an attorney and an accountant. Depending on the type of business and the skills of the owner, from time to time, he may need the advice of other professionals, such as a direct mail or marketing specialist, an insurance representative, management consultant, a computer specialist, a realtor, or a public relations expert.

Several guidelines will hold true no matter what type of expert a business owner deals with: 1) Interview professionals to see if he will be comfortable working with them. Make sure they have served other similar small businesses. Find out ahead of time exactly what service is being purchased, what the working relationship will be, and what fees will be charged. 2) Be completely honest about the business situation. Advice based on partial or incorrect information is no advice at all. If the business is having problems, don't be embarrassed. If the sales are down, give the experts all the available information and work as a team to solve the problem. If business is good, don't be afraid that professionals will steal ideas or expect a raise. Build a trusting, businesslike relationship. 3) Expect the professionals to spend at least some of their time teaching and explaining complex concepts. But don't expect to be spoon-fed or delegate all decisions to them. Take a course at the local community college in recordkeeping and taxes or public relations to develop more skill in areas of inexperience. 4) Keep appointments and pay bills promptly.

To find a lawyer who is familiar with businesses of our size and type, we should ask for referrals from business colleagues, our accountants, the local Chamber of Commerce, our bankers, or some other trusted source. Some local bar associations run a lawyer referral and information service. Some just give names; others actually give information on experience and fees to help match needs to the lawyer's background and charges.

A lawyer can help decide which is the most advantageous business structure (sole proprietorship, partnership, or corporation). He or she can help with zoning, permit, or licensing problems; health inspection problems; unpaid bills; contracts and agreements; patents, trademarks, copyright protection; and some tax problems. Because there is always the possibility of a lawsuit, claim, or other legal action against your business, it is wise to have a lawyer who is already familiar with the business before a crisis arises. A lawyer experienced with our type of ventures could also advise us on laws, programs, and agencies—federal, state and local—that help small businesses through loans, grants, procurement set-asides, counseling, and other ways. He or she can tell us about unexpected legal opportunities and pitfalls that may affect our business.

In choosing a lawyer, experience and fee should be related. One lawyer may charge an hourly rate that, at first, looks cheaper than another lawyer's. However, because of a lack of experience in some area, the less expensive lawyer may charge a larger fee in the long run. Ask for a resumé and check references. If a person feels overwhelmed, he should take a trusted friend to the initial meeting to help him keep on track as he interviews the lawyer about services and fees.

If a law firm is retained, be sure to understand who will work on the case and who will supervise the work. If junior lawyers handle the work, the fees should be lower. That's usually fine as long as an experienced attorney will be reviewing the case periodically.

The business owner should let his lawyer know that he expects to be informed of all developments and consulted before any decisions are made. He may also want to receive copies of all documents, letters, and memos written and received in the case or have a chance to read them in the lawyer's office.

He should ask the attorney to estimate the timetable and costs of the work. He may wish to place a periodic ceiling on fees, after which the attorney would call him before proceeding to do work that would add to the bill. He should always have a written retainer agreement, describing just what he and the lawyer expect of each other.

Most businesses fail not for lack of good ideas or good will, but rather for lack of financial expertise and planning. Business owners should look for an accountant as they would an attorney. The should get referrals from trusted friends, business associations, or professional organizations. They should discuss fees in advance and draw up a written agreement about how they will work together. An accountant (along with a lawyer) can advise about initial business decisions, such as the form of the business. An accountant can also help set up the books, draw up and analyze profit and loss statements, advise on financial decisions, and give advice on cash requirements for the start-up phase. He or she can make budget forecasts, help prepare financial information for a loan application, and handle tax matters.

Accounting firms offer a variety of services. If this is not an easy area for a business owner, the fees he pays will be well worth it. Most firms will maintain books of original entry, prepare bank reconciliation statements and post the general ledger, prepare balance sheets and income statements on a quarterly or semi-annual basis, and design and implement various accounting and recordkeeping systems.

They will also get federal and state withholding numbers, give instructions on where and when to file tax returns, prepare tax returns, and do general tax planning for the small business person.

A business owner's accountant is his key financial advisor. The accountant should alert the owner to potential danger areas and advise him on how to handle growth spurts, how to best plan for slow business times, and how to financially nurture and protect his business future.

Laws That May Apply to Your Business

Most localities have registration and licensing requirements that will apply to business owners. A license is a formal permission to practice a certain business activity, issued by a local, state, or federal government. The activities may be the type of business that requires a permit from the local authorities. There is often a small fee for licenses and permits (usually fifteen to twenty-five dollars). A license may require some kind of examination to certify that the recipient is qualified. The business name must usually be registered and an appropriate tax number must be obtained. Separate business telephones and bank accounts are recommended. If there are employees, the business owner is responsible for withholding income and Social Security taxes. He must also pay worker's compensation and unemployment insurance and comply with minimum wage and employee health laws.

If your operations are intrastate, the business owner will be concerned primarily with state and local, rather than federal, licensing. Businesses frequently subject to state or local control are retail food establishments, drinking places, barber shops, beauty shops, plumbing firms, and taxi companies. They are primarily service businesses and are subject to regulations for the protection of public health and morals. An attorney can help make sure that the owner has complied with all licensing and permit requirements. Depending on the type of business the owner may have to comply with building and safety codes too.

Think twice about the liabilities of operating without proper licenses and registrations. If a business owner begins to advertise or is fortunate enough to "make the news" in some way, he will probably hear from a local official. He will pay with embarrassment, time, and money if his business is not properly licensed.

If the business person finds legal regulations, permits, and licenses confusing, he should make sure he finds some way to get the information he needs to operate legally. He can get help from his lawyer, accountant, business partner, or even his local librarian. This is not an aspect of business operations that can be delayed until the owner "gets around to it." His business reputation and financial standing are at stake.

Learning from Experience and Networking

Successful business owners learn from experience—their own and that of others. In Jeffrey A. Timmon's study of entrepreneurial personality characteristics (*New Venture Creation: A Guide to Small Business Development*), he notes that successful entrepreneurs are disappointed but not discouraged by failure. They use failures as learning experiences and try to understand their role in causing the failure in order to avoid similar problems in the future. Furthermore, Timmons asserts, entrepreneurs seek and use feedback on their performance in order to take corrective action and improve.

As entrepreneurs, we can learn from experience in several ways:

- We can work closely and creatively with professional advisors, such as our lawyers and our accountants. As we continually review our business records, we will see "mistakes," but we will also begin to develop skill in planning and managing.
- We can continue to learn about all areas of business operations, constantly acquiring new ideas. Most community colleges have short, inexpensive, practical courses for business owners in topics like "Financing a Small Business," "Choosing a Small Business Computer," and "Starting and Operating a Home-Based Business."
- We can get to know other business owners with similar needs or problems. Talking with others may be a way to avoid repeating the mistakes they have made and benefiting from their experience. Local and national organizations offer membership, social events, networking opportunities, newsletters, and seminars for small business owners. Through these organizations we can often advertise our product or service to other business owners. They also provide a way to learn about services we may need, such as accounting, public relations, or a responsible secretarial service. These organizations offer updates in such areas as taxes and zoning in their news-letters and workshops.

Whatever the current business problems, there is likely to be a solution. Somewhere there is information, a book, a person, an organization, or a government agency that can help. A word of warning though: finding resources and building networks can be very time-consuming. Joining organizations can turn out to be expensive, especially if the business owner is too busy to use their services and support once he joins. Use the following list or organize a search for useful resources, then pick and choose carefully what to read, join, buy, or attend.

- The Public Library: Visit the local library. Get to know its resources. In addition to books, many libraries offer free workshops, lend skill-building tapes, and become a central place to pick up catalogues and brochures describing continuing education opportunities for business owners. Ask the librarian for current copies of zoning regulations. Get familiar with new books and resources in pertinent fields (computers, health care, crafts, etc.) as well as in business skills (advertising techniques, financing, etc.). Look for magazines such as *In Business, Black Enterprise, Venture*, or *The Journal of Small Business Management*. Reading selectively is free. Subscribing to too many magazines may be expensive.
- Organizations: A wide variety of local and national organizations have sprung up to serve the informational, lobbying, and networking needs of business entrepreneurs. Through meetings, services, or newsletters, groups such as the National Association of Women Business Owners, American Entrepreneurs Association, Business and Professional Women's Club, National Alliance of Homebased Businesswomen, and the National Association for Cottage Industry offer members everything from camaraderie to valuable "perks," such as group rates on health insurance. David Gumpert's book, *The Insider's Guide to Small Business Resources*, has addresses of many of these groups and other information on such resources.

- Government Resources: Contact the local or district office of the U.S. Small Business Administration (SBA) to learn about SBA services and publications. The SBA also offers free or inexpensive workshops and counseling through SCORE®. As mentioned above, SCORE® is a volunteer program sponsored by the SBA through which retired executives who have management expertise are linked with owners/managers of small business or prospective entrepreneurs who need help.

The Department of Commerce, Bureau of the Census, Department of Defense (procurement), Department of Labor, IRS (ask for the free "Business Tax Kit"), Federal Trade Commission, and the Government Printing Office all have publications and services to inform and support small businesses. Local and state government offices may also provide services and assistance. Addresses will be available in the telephone book, under U.S. Government, at the public library, or at the SBA office.

- Community colleges: Most community colleges now have short, inexpensive, noncredit programs for entrepreneurs. The classes usually are convenient to business owners and are taught by experienced owners and managers.

If a person is a small business person, particularly if operating out of his home, he can overcome feelings of isolation and give and receive valuable information if he taps into networks and resources. Being active in professional and trade associations will help to build a good marketing network for the business' service or product. Take the time and invest the money for memberships. Then continually evaluate which organizations and resources best serve business information and networking needs.

SMART MANEUVERS

PART TWO

DEVELOPING CAREER SKILLS

CHAPTER SIX

BECOMING PROFICIENT WITH COMPUTERS

*N*o longer can we afford to let our skills and personal development stagnate. Remaining competitive and finding success in our careers and personal endeavors will require that we constantly assess our strengths and weaknesses and take measures to foster our growth and development. In the high-tech world of today and tomorrow, we must become proficient with computers to maintain our efficiency and effectiveness on and off the job. Our success will also depend on acquiring effective communication and negotiation skills. All of us need to take full advantage of available training, skills development courses, and other continuing education programs to ensure our marketability in the information age.

Making Use of Computers

In 1973, the microcomputer was invented. Within a short period of time, computers began showing up in the classrooms of America. In 1981, only eighteen percent of all public elementary and secondary schools in the U.S. used computers in their instruction. By 1990, nearly ninety-eight percent of public schools were using computers. As pervasive as computers have become in the schools, the U.S. Department of Energy reported only sixteen percent of all U.S. households had a personal computer in 1990. However, by the end of 1993 the personal computer had become one of the fastest selling items within our economy, and an estimated thirty percent of all households had one.

There is a fascination with computers in our society. Computers are everywhere, they are doing everything, and we have come to expect nothing less. Having a personal computer, for some people, is being in vogue. Using a personal computer will increase our ability to retrieve and recall information because a computer's memory is more complete and exact than our own. And using a computer will increase our organizational and technical skills (e.g., spelling, grammar, graphs, and math). Unquestionably, by having and using a computer, our smartness, perceived or actual, can be enhanced. Becoming proficient with personal computers and using them in our professional and personal lives will be a timely and smart maneuver. No one can realistically expect to be successful in our world of mega-information without being able to use a computer.

The ways we can use a computer in our businesses, homes, education, and personal affairs are unlimited. For example, some typical ways we can make effective use of computers in our work or business include: bringing work home from the office, personalizing form letters, financial planning, and accounting or statistical analysis. We can keep client and other business lists for quick sorting into categories or for mailings. We can create charts, graphs, presentations; manage projects; make a business plan; keep an inventory; and forecast future expenses and earnings.

We can use the computer for educational purposes for accessing encyclopedias and other research data; searching remote data banks; learning math, reading, foreign languages, typing, and other subjects; and preparing for college entrance. Computers are useful in home management for budgeting and balancing checkbooks; tax return preparation; storing and sorting the family calendar, Christmas card list, and favorite recipes; and keeping a household inventory. We can make personal use of our computers for writing letters and resumés; writing a book, a short story, or a poem; personal financial management; tracking the stock market; and shopping. We can access our bank account to transfer funds, pay bills, or check our balance. The computer can help us find the cheapest airfare and book our tickets. We can stay in contact with other computer owners, and even automate our homes.

Additionally, we can use the computer in many specialty projects such as making signs and labels; preparing presentation graphics; and designing bridges, buildings, and the like. Computers can be used in publishing books, pamphlets, and newsletters (desktop publishing); composing music; and drawing and painting. There is no part of our professional or personal lives that can not, and will not, be impacted by computers.

An important question is, how proficient should we become, and how can we go about achieving the required level of skill for effectively using a computer? One way to achieve basic computer literacy is through an introductory computer course. These courses are available at many colleges, trade schools, continuing education programs, and through employer-sponsored training. An introductory computer course can explain the component parts of a computer system, and offer examples on basic ways of using them. It can also provide an insight on present, future, and historical uses of the computer.

We can usually learn how to operate the basic computer equipment, such as the keyboard, mouse, printers, and other peripheral devices, through the factory owner's manuals. Manufacturers in the computer industry have made a concerted effort to write "user friendly" instructions on the use of their products. Software suppliers provide publications and other accompanying manuals, which instruct us on nearly every aspect of the software's capabilities and how we can use them. With a general understanding of hardware and software, we can use computers to perform word processing, calculations, graphics, desktop publishing, fax transmissions, and a variety of other functions mentioned earlier.

The secret to becoming proficient with a computer is to

become smart about information and the software that handles it. We must fully appreciate what information really is: meaningful data which assists us in understanding and decision-making. Software must be selected which will collect and manage data that will make our information complete and understandable. We should always keep in mind that computers are merely instruments which manage meaningful data better and faster than we could manually. It is up to us to decide what information is important to manage and how we might make the most effective use of computers.

The Value of Information

Information is an essential resource for success. We are in the midst of an information explosion, a phenomenon so great that it is changing the very nature of our society and our perspective on the world. We have been propelled from an industrial society to an information society in just twenty years. Our economy is now completely dependent on the production, management, and use of information. We are bombarded with details and facts continually. But, what we need for performance and overall success is information that is focused to the tasks we perform and the decisions we make everyday.

Without question, the personal computer can be an effective tool for accumulating facts and reshaping them into usable information. Important details of our professional and personal lives can be assembled to keep us knowledgeable and informed.

Alone, data such as details and facts are meaningless; they must be changed to a usable form and placed in context to have informational value. Data becomes information when it is transformed to communicate meaning, knowledge, ideas, or conclusions. Otherwise, data is just an abbreviation or a code representing something. Information, then, is really knowledge based on data that has been given meaning, purpose, and usefulness.

In order to be valuable to us, information must have certain attributes. Information must be relevant, accurate, and timely. Being bombarded with unlimited and indiscriminate information is unlikely to assist us in our functions. Instead we can become paralyzed with trying to analyze too much irrelevant information. It is important that we determine our information needs and set up measures to provide the information which will be of value to us.

Relevance is a key factor contributing to the value of information. Not all data or facts are relevant at a given moment. Indeed, some information we receive may never be relevant to any task or decision-making that we perform. The computer can play a major role in helping us analyze the universe of information to determine whether it is meaningful and relevant to us the user.

Information must be accurate in order for us to make effective use of it. Accuracy describes whether information represents a situation, level, or state of an event as it really is. Information which is inaccurate will cause us to make erroneous decisions. The burden of accuracy usually rests with the provider of the information, and adequate steps must be taken to prevent errors during collecting and entering information.

Having enough space for filing documents has always been a serious concern for well-structured offices. Paper documents, in large file cabinets, not only make storage difficult, but the files are also hard to maintain and research. A personal computer condenses hundreds of documents on magnetic disks. This makes it easier to decide what information is valuable and can be kept. The answer is that virtually every document we make can be stored on hard or floppy disks and managed with ease using computers. The computer offers today's children the ability to retain every document they create during their lives on a few magnetic or optical disks (optical disks eventually will replace magnetic disks or tapes). With the unlimited possibilities that will accompany the information superhighway of the near future, a person can never have too much storage capacity.

Using a computer to handle information is called data

processing. Almost every job function we will ever perform will involve some kind of information handling or data processing. Data processing can be performed manually—with the help of a keydriven device such as a pocket calculator or typewriter—or with a computer. In all cases, the processing consists of one or more operations involving recording, sorting, sequencing, arranging, merging, calculating, storing, retrieving, reproducing, or displaying data for the intended users. Using computers to perform these tasks will allow us to handle data with speed, accuracy and dependability.

Understanding Computer Software

Software is the most important part of our computer systems. Software is the general term describing programs of instructions, languages, and routines or procedures that make it possible for us to use the computer. The term is often applied only to commercially-prepared packages, as opposed to user-prepared instructions. Commercially prepared programs are developed by manufacturers or companies that specialize in software. Most users of personal computers have at least three types of productive software: word processing, electronic spreadsheets, and a data base management system. A fourth category, desktop publishing, is rapidly gaining popularity. These categories of productive software are referred to as software applications or application software. Their primary purpose is to control all processing activities and to make sure that the resources and power of the computer are used in the most efficient manner.

Word Processing: The applications of word processing software are almost endless. Word processing is a computerized approach to creating, editing, revising, storing, and printing documents. Word processing software assists the user in assembling memos, letters, reports, and other written forms. It allows us to create documents, revise them, and print out the finished version with relative ease. The revision stage is much more efficient than in the past since words, phrases, and even para-

110

graphs can be changed, moved, or deleted without having to retype the entire document. Form documents can be prepared and used over and over again, with just a name or phrase changed here and there. Documents can be copied, pasted, and merged to create reports or other personalized materials for a specific use with little or no effort.

Electronic Spreadsheets: Electronic spreadsheets aid in the accumulation of number facts. From the moment this type of software was released to the public in 1979, computer spreadsheet applications were an immediate success. One of the primary uses of spreadsheets is to build models to analyze financial or other numerical situations and to explore the effects that changes have on the outcome. This application offers us the ability to examine a series of "what-if" scenarios where we can look at several alternatives simply by changing certain key figures and letting the program recalculate the results.

Data Base Management: The real value of any data base management program is how easily we can retrieve information and conduct a sophisticated information search. When we first create a database file, we have to tell the program what fields we plan on storing data in so that it can allocate space for them. This step is called defining the data base. When we define a data base, we describe each field by specifying its name, length, and the type of data to be stored. By defining the content of the data base and planning exactly what information is to be included in the fields of each record, we are in control of what information is important enough to keep. Data base management software allows users to store information in any form, with the benefit of fast retrieval. There is a growing use of data base programs that permit integration of pictures and graphic displays with data.

Desktop Publishing: One of the most exciting developments in computer applications has been the birth of a new industry—desktop publishing. Often, when preparing reports and other kinds of documents, it is necessary to include graphics to illustrate ideas. Desktop publishing software and a laser printer will enable us to produce material that includes both graphics and text and looks like it was printed professionally. Traditionally, graphic illustration was prepared separately and then inserted or pasted in. Now, it is possible to print graphics right in the document.

While desktop publishing applications are recognized for their ability to mix graphics and text and perform the complicated and time-consuming task of page composition and layout, they are ideally suited for many practical applications that people may not think of as desktop publishing. Specialized uses of desktop publishing include the printing of sheet music and scientific papers with mathematical or chemical formulas. Basically, desktop publishing can be used to publish an endless variety of professional-looking documents.

Software is being designed to make the computer easier to use. It is possible to purchase a variety of software applications to handle our important information. We should keep in mind that each software package could handle our data differently. So, smart purchases must be planned and studied. The software's packaging provides a wealth of information on compatibility and features. Compatibility is important because it allows us to use our data with other software applications. We can begin our reading with the software's package, and seek guidance from consumer related reports or computer professionals to give us a better understanding of what we should be purchasing.

Steps to Using Computer Software

An important part of becoming proficient with our computer is becoming familiar with our software. A helpful way to look at software applications is to envision software usage as five basic steps. Envisioning software in this manner will lessen the anxiety of learning every aspect of the software's programs right away. These steps are:

- Knowing how to begin the program: A person should know how to turn the program on, and how to enter information on the screen. Each software package has explicit instructions on how to get started. Taking time to become acquainted with how to move around the screen, change fonts, and enter data, is worthwhile. Going through the tutorial which accompanies most software is also helpful.

- Knowing how to save information: Knowing how to save information is crucial while using computers. Periodically, as we work, we should take the precaution of saving documents under a name that identifies the substance of the information within. Knowing how to save our work on floppy disks is also important. It will always be helpful to have a portable copy of our information. Naming records and files, with words which relate to its content, should become a habit. Taking the time upfront to provide information on the content, authorship, and date will facilitate easy retrieval later.

- Knowing how to print information: Since the Chinese invented paper in 105 A.D., it has been the most popular medium for presenting thoughts and ideas. Getting information onto paper, with a computer, requires an understanding of the dimensions of the paper and how to use layout and print functions effectively. Our software print options will determine the ultimate appearance of our work.

- Knowing how to retrieve information: We must be able to gain access to documents and files to make effective use of our computers. Computer software has become friendlier and more effective in displaying the names of records and files worked on and saved.

- Knowing how to exit the software: When ending the computer session, certain steps should be routinely taken to avoid damage to our systems. The computer software does a lot more behind the scenes than most of us are aware of. Besides closing files, application software must communicate with operating software which controls the computer's peripheral devices—like printers and the mouse. The proper exit procedures release the computer's resources, save records, and close files. We should always follow the software's recommended procedures for ending a session.

Acquiring Computer Skills and Equipment

If we do not know how to use a computer, our future success can be in jeopardy until we learn. If we are presently using a computer, our skills will naturally increase to a level of competency and comfort over time. But, to become a skilled user of this technology, we must think about how the computer can organize and manage the information we use and require to perform tasks and decision-making. Once we have identified our major uses of a computer, then we can resolve issues such as:

- Which computer will work best with the software we need?
- How much memory should our computer have?
- Which operating system is best for us?
- Whether we need a full-sized personal computer, a laptop, or an even smaller computer?

Communicating with others, in the very near future, will be done in digital form, transmitted over fiber optic cable or radio wave frequencies. The proposed information superhighway will facilitate the intricate paths to information banks and networks. With the advent of this new information highway, we will be able to reach rich sources of information like libraries, research institutions, and other computer users. The sources of information that will be accessible on the information superhighway will eventually encompass all of mankind's knowledge.

Acquiring the right computer hardware and software and keeping it up-to-date is important in maximizing the utility of our computers. Minimum hardware recommendations include a letter quality printer (impact or laser), a color monitor, a telecommunication's modem, a keyboard and a mouse, and the central processing unit (CPU). The fullest use of a personal computer will require the ability to communicate with other computers and is dependent upon a modem and the appropriate telecommunication hardware.

Beyond the hardware, we should also be aware of what software is worth having. Because of the abundance of software packages available in today's market, choosing the right software can tailor our data processing for the greatest ease and convenience. We should consider special-purpose software instead of "reinventing the wheel." Ease and convenience in using our personal computer will improve our proficiency on our systems.

There are many sources of information about computers that are available to us. Here's how to take advantage of them:

- Visit a user's group (a computer information-sharing club of people who own the same brand and model computer). Computer retailers have lists of them.
- Read newspaper columns, books, and magazines devoted to personal computers. Libraries, newsstands, and bookstores are good sources.
- Take a course offered by a computer retailer or a local school.
- Attend a computer show. Check computer retailers or newspapers for date, place, and time.
- Check with friends or business associates who use computers.
- Write to computer manufacturers for information.
- Read directories and reviews of software and look over software publisher's catalogs available from computer dealers.

CHAPTER SEVEN

COMMUNICATING EFFECTIVELY

*E*ffective communication is the language of professional and personal success. We are unlikely to find fulfillment in life unless we are able to express our ideas and feelings, and listen carefully to others.

Communication is normally thought of as simply speaking and writing. But communication is a complex process engaged in by at least two people for the exchange of information. All parties to the communication process must be keenly alert if the process is to be successful.

The sender uses verbal, written, and visual means to convey the message. The receiver uses auditory and visual skills to decode the message. Speaking, reading, hearing, seeing—all are part of the communication process. How we send a message depends on our tone, demeanor, posture and other factors. In written communication our writing style and clarity will invariably affect how our message is received. Our ability to master written and oral communication will be an important key to our success and overall happiness.

Writing for Success

Today's professionals are perhaps the most prolific writers of all times. Our output of letters, reports, memoranda and so on is staggering—and in many cases ineffective. Malcolm Forbes, former president and CEO of *Forbes Magazine*, estimated that over 10,000 letters alone crossed his desk in any given year. He classified them into three categories: 1) stultifying (if not stupid), 2) mundane (most of the 10,000 fell into this category), and 3) first rate (a very rare breed of them).

In professional writing, it is important that we arrange our thoughts and present our ideas clearly. The cost of confusion from written communications can be high in the professional world. Foggy writing eats up the reading time of highly paid executives, creates misunderstanding and errors, and often makes it necessary to do the job over at additional costs. Clarity, as well as time, is invaluable. Keep in mind that business people read selectively and do a great deal of scanning. Therefore, for effective business writing, we must make our points concisely, conspicuously, and plainly.

We should examine each of our writings with the idea of improving it. We should do so as a mark of respect for ourselves and the reader. If we scribble our thoughts chaotically, our readers will surely feel that we care little about them or ourselves. People will judge us by the way we write.

Here are some practical hints each of us can follow for being effective with business and professional writings:

- Know what you want to say: You cannot write clearly unless, before you start, you know where you will stop. Think of writing as a trip from a definite start to a definite destination. Before you begin to write you should have a clear idea of the points you intend to make and the order in which you mean to make them. Prepare an outline before you write. It is the lack of an outline that makes so much business writing flabby, formless, and hard to follow.

  Write down in one sentence what you want the results of your writing to be. Then list all the major points that need to be addressed. Keep the letter in front of you while you write. Also start where your readers are. Ask yourself, "How much do they know about the subject?"

- Be direct and to the point: Explain what your letter, memo or report is about in the first paragraph. Put important points first. Do not keep the reader guessing or he or she might file your letter or report away even before she finishes it. For lengthy reports, begin each paragraph with a simple, declarative topic sentence that sums up what is to follow. This makes for clearer thinking as well as fast, easy reading. Write accurately and concisely, always selecting the most effective words.

  Bear in mind when you are choosing words and putting them together, how they sound. People read with their eyes, but actually hear what they are reading in their heads.
- Keep it simple: Successful people, people at the top, usually write in clear, simple language. Clutter is a disease in most writing. The natural tendency is to inflate and thereby sound important. Simplicity is the most effective approach even with complex subject matter. Use plain English and avoid acronyms and technical jargon.
- Edit your writing: If a sentence, no matter how excellent, does not illuminate your subject matter in some new and useful way, scratch it out. The more words you use, the less each is worth. Go through your writing as many times as it takes. Annihilate unnecessary words, sentences—even paragraphs. Check your grammar and spelling.
- Keep your writing organized: Break up long stretches of solid writing with sub-captions and headings. Use paragraphing that makes it easy to read and tabulate your main points. Make sure that your writing flows smoothly from one point to the next. Use a format which is effective in keeping the reader's interest and which highlights the points you are making.
- Sum up your writing: End your paper or each main division of it with a summary paragraph. In letters, the last paragraph should tell the reader exactly what you want him to do—or what you are going to do.

These principles apply to business memos, letters, reports, and proposals as well as any other kind of professional writing. Following them will help us to write simply, clearly, and successfully.

Effective Speaking and Presentation

More people have talked their way up the ladder of success than have climbed it in any other way. This underscores the importance of effective speaking and presentation skills. It also emphasizes the need for us to develop excellent speaking abilities and to use these skills to foster our career and personal success.

What does it take to be an effective speaker? How can we learn to speak with power and impact? It starts by knowing the purpose of the presentation and the intended audience.

Keep in mind that every public speaking situation is made up of four major components: speaker, speech, audience, and occasion. Each of these affects the other and the success of the presentation. If the speech is well written, yet the delivery unpolished, it takes away from the speaker achieving his or her purpose. If we can't communicate a message, it doesn't matter how brilliant the message is.

The three basic purposes of speech are to inform, persuade, or entertain. Each type of speech has different methods of organization and different types of supporting materials. Understanding the purpose of our presentation can help us prepare and deliver a successful one.

Before preparing a presentation, it is essential that we know to whom we are talking. An analysis of the audience will often dictate the approach and content of our presentation. We should design our presentation for the specific group or audience that we want to reach.

What we say and how we say it frequently depend on the occasion. We should always understand the occasion and make sure our presentation fits.

Following these principles will help each of us deliver successful presentations:

- Know the purpose (inform, persuade, or entertain): An informative presentation should contain new and useful information for the audience. If the information is not new to the audience, and has no other knowledge or awareness benefit, it does not perform the function of informing. To inform, a speech should instruct, not merely help an audience pass the time. New and useful information can best be learned when it is organized in a meaningful pattern.

  Informative speeches should contain elements which will make the audience want to learn the information in the speech. People learn best when they are motivated to do so. In our introductions we should point out the importance of the information to our audiences and then relate our subject matter to their needs, wants, and desires throughout our speeches.

  Persuasive speaking has the purpose of causing people to take action to change their attitudes or beliefs, or to reinforce their attitudes or beliefs. To persuade audiences we have three basic approaches: persuading through evidence and reasoning; persuading through emotional and psychological needs, wants, and desires; and persuading through our own credibility as a speaker. In almost all cases of successful persuasion, these three methods are usually mixed in varying degrees, depending on the speaker's analysis of his or her audience, character, and style.

  Know the audience (attitudes, needs, demographics): Of vital importance to successful speaking is knowing the audience. Whether we speak to a large or a small group, we should study our audiences in order to determine how they may feel and think about us and our subject. Each audience will be different and we will have to consider many factors.

The way we use language and examples, the way we frame main points, and the way we illustrate them will be affected by demographic characteristics such as age, sex, education, occupation, and socio-economic status. Information about religion, cultural/ethnic breakdowns, political affiliation and group membership may also be valuable in many situations.

- Know the logistics: A successful presentation can be greatly impacted by the size of the audience, length of the presentation, time of day, and other logistical factors.
- Organize the presentation: Set up the presentation in a way that the audience will find easy to follow. People have a need for logic and comprehension. We should provide this by selecting a method of organization which our audience can understand.

Here are some typical organization formats for presentations:

Chronological: Time sequence of events are involved. For example, discussing our educational development from pre-school to post doctorate.

Spatial or geographical: For example, sights to see in western Europe.

Topical: Taking a large topic and breaking it into subtopics. For example, types of equity loans offered by local banks.

Comparison and contrast: For example, discussing various options for solving a problem.

Cause and effect: A presentation on what has or will happen and finding a cause or a result.

Problem to solution: A need for change is recognized and a solution is presented.

Proposition to proof: Involves presenting our propositions and then proving them through the body of our speech. We conclude with an appeal to accept or act upon our propositions.

Whatever our organizational format, our presentations should follow the basic format of introducing the audience to what we are going to say, saying it, and then summarizing what we said. We should limit our presentation to about three main topics, or we could quickly lose our audience.

• Support the presentation: Include information, facts, statistics, examples, testimony, humor, and visual aids. We can use these to substantiate our viewpoint, clarify a point, make a point interesting; and to get the audience alert, thoughtful, involved and observant, as well as make the presentation memorable.

• Keep the audience's attention: Develop a receptive atmosphere and a good rapport with the audience. We should use interesting techniques for getting the attention of our audience in the introduction of our speech. For example we can ask a question; state an unusual fact; present a quotation; refer to an historic event; tell a joke; use a gimmick; point to common relationships, beliefs, interests, or opinions; refer to the occasion, purpose of the meeting, audience, or some other part of the program; compliment the audience; or point out the extreme importance of the subject to the audience.

• Close the presentation: Summarize and end the presentation for lasting impact. We could consider returning to the attention-getter that we used at the start, but now with a different ending, or additional line, or another insight or explanation. Equally effective is to look to the future. Pointing to the future extends to our audience the invitation to consider, explore, and think further about our subject.

CHAPTER EIGHT

NEGOTIATING SUCCESSFULLY

*W*hen people are asked what "negotiation" means to them there are usually a wide variety of answers. Some people think of union-management disputes and collective bargaining. Others think of athletes as they hold out for bigger and bigger salaries, international peace talks, or trade negotiations. The fact is we negotiate every day. Any time we deal with another person to obtain something that we want, we are negotiating.

We negotiate at work with supervisors, co-workers, customers, suppliers, government officials; at home with our spouse, parents, children, neighbors, and friends; and elsewhere with sales people, auto dealers, merchants, and others. Being able to negotiate effectively is an important part of professional and personal success.

Approaches to Negotiation

Historically, there have been two basic styles of negotiation—the "hard," positional approach and the "soft," relational approach. The hard, positional approach focuses on taking an extreme initial position, and compromising as little as possible through a succession of give-and-take. The soft, relational approach focuses on friendship, trust, and a desire to reach agreement on nearly any terms to preserve the relationship. Although the soft approach is effective in many situations, it is vulnerable to the hard approach and will likely lose to it.

The traditional approaches to negotiation offer fertile ground for the innovative negotiator. The new negotiator strives for what is referred to as "win-win" outcomes where all parties involved can have their needs met while their pride and ego remain intact. This negotiation style is often referred to as "principle negotiating." It requires skill, thought, and creativity. It make it possible to keep the relationship of the parties intact—since in most instances the negotiation process does not end the parties' contact with each other, but begins a continuing relationship on new terms.

The ability to negotiate successfully requires creativity and good people-skills. It also requires persistence, endurance, patience, organization, risk-taking, vision, and high ethical values. Nearly everyone can be an effective negotiator given the right preparation and knowledge of negotiating principles.

Three basic principles emerge from studying top negotiators. The first principle is "be soft on people, hard on ideas." This means that, as negotiators, we should separate emotions from issues. This will help maintain a cooperative relationship between both parties. The second principle is to focus our attention on the major relevant issues and the desires and intentions behind the issues. The objective here is to discover what each party really wants, so that we can understand the actual needs of the parties and seek alternatives which will satisfy those needs. The third principle is to create multiple options to help reach an agreement. There are many ways to reach a final agreement. The basis for successful negotiation is to be highly flexible and prolific in generating options.

The Elements of Successful Negotiation

There are seven elements which are important in achieving effective negotiations. These are alternatives, intentions, options, legitimacy, communication, relationship, and commitment. Let's take a look of these elements and the role each plays in making each of us a successful negotiator.

- Alternatives: The first element of successful negotiation is that an agreement through negotiation be better than the alternatives. If any of the alternatives to a negotiated agreement is better than the agreement we might negotiate, there is no point in negotiating. However, if there are no alternatives to a negotiated agreement, the pressure to reach an agreement, any agreement, is high. This high-intensity situation makes for a weak negotiating position. Lower intensity allows a person to be more resourceful and in control of the negotiating process. The goal is to reduce the intensity by generating, increasing, and improving our alternatives to a negotiated agreement. This is what Roger Fisher, director of the Harvard Negotiation Project, calls developing our "Best Alternative To a Negotiated Agreement" (BATNA).

There are essentially two ways to develop or improve our BATNA. The first method is to increase the number of parties or entities that can satisfy what we want from a negotiated agreement. If the party we are negotiating with is the only one that can satisfy what we want, the intensity will be high. If we seek out and find other parties that can meet or come close to satisfying our intentions, the intensity will be greatly reduced.

The second method involves changing the time constraint. The time constraint is the amount of time remaining before we will begin to experience negative consequences from not having an agreement. If we have to have an agreement today, our negotiating position is considerably weaker than if we have six months to reach an agreement. The best way to handle the time constraint is to extend our time by starting our negotiation process as early as possible.

- Intentions: Effective negotiation requires that the intentions of all the parties be acceptably satisfied. Initially, this element may seem ironic. How can everybody be satisfied? Somebody has to give while the other receives. According to traditional game theory, every gain by one party must equivalently correspond to a loss by the opposing party. While this outcome may apply to certain types of games, it has no place in successful negotiations.

Effective negotiations are fostered by first discovering the stated intentions of each party and then eliciting the unconscious intentions. This element is also effectively used during the negotiation planning stage before meeting with the other party. This pre-planning is absolutely vital to being successful in any negotiation.

- Options: The third element of effective negotiations is that the best options be identified and pursued. Here is where creativity is an asset during both the planning stage and actual negotiations to create many options that can satisfy both parties. During the negotiations, we can use the information that we learn about the parties' intentions to make "can-do" propositions. A "can-do" proposition is one that satisfies our intentions well, and acceptably satisfies the intentions of the other party such that there is a reasonable chance the other party will say yes to it.

- Legitimacy: The element of legitimacy is essential so that none of the parties feel they have been taken advantage of. Legitimacy requires the use of reasonable and objective standards, such as fair market values, current standard procedures, and the like, in setting demands and expectations. The use of objective standards serves to separate the issues from the people. When objective standards are used as a base to formulate positions the importance of personality fades as well as the risk of emotional conflict. This also preserves the long-term relationships and establishes a positive atmosphere for the next negotiations.

- Communication: Effective negotiation requires that there be good communication between the parties. The basis of good communication is building rapport with the other party. In order to establish rapport quickly with another person we must know how to pace behaviors. Pacing is matching ourselves with the verbal and non-verbal behavior of another person to establish rapport. An underlying principle behind the effectiveness of pacing is that we are more easily influenced by a person that we perceive as similar to ourselves. The more similarity that exist between ourselves and someone, the more likely we are to draw the conclusion that the person is predictable. The more predictable a person is, the less stress we experience in our attempts to negotiate with that person. Understanding how communication and pacing affects the relationship between two people is one of the primary skills of a good negotiator. We can be polite and still be a tough negotiator. Being argumentative is unlikely to help the negotiation process. Good negotiators are active listeners.

- Relationship: A successful negotiation requires that the relationship between the parties be improved by the negotiation or at least not damaged. Remember that the negotiated agreement provides the basis for the beginning of a continuing future involvement with the other party. By operating with a state of mind focused on relationship building, we will discover that this is a powerful tool which can enhance the negotiation process.

- Commitment: The final element of a successful negotiation is that realistic commitments are made. Unless the commitments are realistic, well understood, and easy for all parties to carry out, they will likely cause future difficulties and require further negotiations.

Planning for a Successful Negotiation

Without planning and information-gathering a person will be at a disadvantage in any negotiation. Nowhere is the saying "information is power" more emphatic than in the art of negotiation. All other things being equal, the negotiating party with the most knowledge and information about his or her opponent has the advantage.

Often times in negotiation each side has an intimate understanding of his or her perspective coming to the negotiating table, but neither side has an understanding of the perspective of the other. However, understanding the other party's perspective enables good negotiators to make certain educated predictions about the response of the other party to any proposals which may be made. This advance intelligence is invaluable in negotiations because it assists us in drafting proposals and options that have a good chance of being accepted.

We should prepare for negotiations by learning as much as possible about our situation and our opponents. Research the other parties' history, previous agreements, and bargaining style. Get to know the other parties informally, if possible, before the negotiations start. Remember, successful negotiators get information about the other party by shifting their perceptional positions—actually seeing and hearing through the eyes and ears of the other party.

We should try to answer the following questions about ourselves and the other party when planning for negotiation:

- What is our emotional intensity? In other words, how badly do we need this agreement? Is it our job, our position, our pride? What factors contribute to our emotional intensity?
- What is our best alternative to a negotiated agreement (BATNA)? Do we have any alternatives to getting this agreement? What will happen if we do not get an agreement?
- What is our time constraint? By what date do we have to have an agreement? When will we start to experience negative consequences if we do not get an agreement?
- What are our intentions? What specifically do we want to get out of these negotiations?
- What are our unconscious intentions? If we were to get what we want, what would that do for us? What would it really accomplish?
- Are there any other parties that can satisfy what we want other than the one we are going to negotiate with? Is there

any other way for us to get what we want other than having to negotiate with this party?

The answers to these questions will give us deep insight into our state of mind and that of the other party. Collecting information about the other party and about the situation using perceptual shifts is vital. This means continually shifting perspective, putting ourselves in the other parties' position, so that we know as much as possible about them. If we fail to do this, we will be operating only from a single view of the situation—our own perspective and feelings. Such an information deficit will likely lead to untargeted and unsuccessful negotiations.

Option analysis is another negotiation planning tool. It is our best estimate of how the other party will perceive his or her choices going into the negotiations. To create an option analysis, we should first formulate the options that will satisfy our interests, and to which we would like the other party to say yes. We should then do positional shifts to gain the other party's perspective and likely response to the proposed options. This is extremely valuable information as it provides us with information to rework the options. The use of option analysis will provide a wealth of information that allows tremendous flexibility in creating options for can-do propositions—options that satisfy the interest for both parties.

As stated earlier, having no alternatives to a negotiated agreement puts us in a very weak negotiating position. Having a good BATNA will keep us out of that "have to make a deal—any deal" feeling. It allows us to keep our emotional intensity low and resourcefulness high—a very useful state of mind to be in when we are in negotiations. It is also a safety net that can prevent us from falling into an unwise agreement. During the course of developing a BATNA we will become familiar with exactly what our interests are, and be better able to recognize what will satisfy those interests and what will not. Our ability to calmly judge the situation is enhanced. We become better negotiators.

We should prepare for negotiations by establishing our

opening position, our target, and our bottom line position. We should be ready to explain our position. We need to develop a good negotiating plan beforehand.

The Negotiation Process

Start the negotiation process by establishing a positive negotiating climate. Be casual, friendly and relaxed, and try to get the other party to do the same. Prepare an agenda and review the rules of the negotiation. We can start the negotiation moving by discussing and trying to reach agreement on the minor issues. The major issues can be addressed later, when we and the other party have developed a rapport and a positive climate.

After both parties have outlined what they want out of the negotiations, it is time to begin generating options that will satisfy the interest of both parties. Now that the parties' intentions are on the table, options can be invented using a procedural method called "brainstorming." Brainstorming is a method for collaboratively inventing multiple options any combination of which could form the basis for an eventual agreement.

For brainstorming to work effectively it must be crafted carefully. Two rules must be followed during the process. First, no negative comments are allowed in response to any ideas put forth no matter how improbable or illogical they may appear. Second, it must be acknowledged by both parties that ideas brought forth during brainstorming are not to be construed as commitments in any form. When brainstorming is well conducted, it can be an amazingly creative experience in which two apparently crazy ideas can spawn a third brilliant one.

In the traditional form of "hard" negotiating, a series of positions are taken and then given up. Often this becomes a test of determination to see who can hang onto their positions the longest. Positions are given up in the smallest of increments and the process can be very time consuming and emotionally fraying. This negotiating process focuses on what each side is willing to agree to. Our wills are pitted against theirs. In this test of wills no negotiation is likely to have an amicable result, nor a result that is in the interest of both parties. The alternative to this approach is to negotiate, not on the basis of what each party is subjectively willing to agree to, but to negotiate on the basis of some reasonable and objective standard apart from the emotional wills of the parties.

As mentioned earlier, negotiating on the basis of objective standards has several advantages. First, it removes the battle for dominance that takes place in most negotiations where each side tries to force the other to back down from their position. In this way, it reduces the potential for escalating conflict. Even if we cannot agree on what the objective standards should be, we can agree to search for some objective standards that are fair to both parties. This agreement alone represents a commitment to fairness that will enhance the working relationship between parties. In turn, this improves the chances for an agreement that meets the interest of both sides. Another advantage to using objective standards is that it helps to insure that neither party is "shafted" or "taken." It helps in preserving a working relationship and is important where long-term relationships are important to both parties.

In summary here is a step-by-step procedure for conducting and concluding successful negotiations.

- Handle the relationship by establishing a cooperative climate; agreeing on the ground rules; agreeing on an agenda; and identifying mutual outcomes.
- Discover the real problems by identifying the problems and restating them in positive and resolvable terms. In difficult situations, move-on up by focusing on a broader and broader vision.
- Establish criteria by identifying outside objective standards and individual expectations.
- Generate multiple options and evaluate these options using established criteria. Agree on the best option for each issue, and then develop, enhance, and refine best options.
- Obtain closure by summarizing specific areas of agree-

133

ment. Establish action plans for completion with time frames and accountability. If no agreement, summarize consequences and options.

- Acknowledge others participating in the negotiation and thank them for their contribution. Reinforce the desire for a win-win situation and a long-term relationship.

Handling Conflict in Negotiations

Negotiation is often defined as the resolution of opposing interests. For example, one party wants a price increase while the other party wants a price decrease—both interests in apparent opposition to one another. This often leads to conflict in a negotiation which will destroy the process if not properly managed. The escalation of conflict has identifiable stages and the ability to discern these stages is the key to avoiding and managing conflict in negotiations.

Learn to recognize the five stages of conflict escalation:

- Proliferation of issues: When conflict begins to escalate, the first transformation to occur is the proliferation of issues. What starts out as a single issue of disagreement becomes multiple issues. Emotions build at this stage while more and more issues are brought into the fray.
- Personal assault on character: The second transformation in the escalation of conflict occurs when the discussion issues turn into personal assaults on character.
- Coercive tactics: The tactics used by both sides of the conflict move from light to heavy. Early tactics used in conflict are usually persuasive in nature, but at this stage they become coercive.
- Prevail at any cost: Before conflict, getting what one can is the goal and usually the motivation in negotiations. At this stage, however, the motivation changes to prevailing in any way you can. The attitude is "when all is lost, make sure that if there is a hell below we're all going to go." At this stage all vestiges of rationality can disappear.

- Involvement of others: In the last stage of escalation of conflict other people become involved in the conflict to help resolve issues. One party attempts to go over the other party's head or seek other avenues for redress.

To be successful negotiators we need to understand and be able to recognize conflict when it occurs. Early recognition of conflict escalation puts us in a position to reverse the direction.

Following some basic principles can help us manage conflict in negotiations. There is no such thing as a win-lose situation for either party. We either win-win or lose-lose. We should give the opposing party time to think over his or her position. We should not try to rush the decision. None of the parties should be regarded as wrong. Conflict arises when we project our values on others. Avoid sarcasm or abrupt statements, judgments, or opinions. Listen without interrupting. Always listen for intent as well as content.

Successful negotiations and conflict management requires that we be able to effectively handle emotions. The key to handling emotions is gathering information about the concern that spawned the emotions, and then encouraging full expression of the emotions. If we hear emotion-laden statements during negotiations, it is time to halt the forward motion of the negotiations, discover the source of the emotions, and encourage expression of concerns. Trying to solve the concern or generate solutions without fully acknowledging and understanding the source of the emotions typically will result in unsatisfactory solutions.

Many times we assume that we know enough about the situation, but until we have encouraged the other party to completely express their feelings surrounding the concern, this is not the case. People seldom express their feelings fully or state their concerns precisely without encouragement and guidance. Instead, they express the problem in small pieces, and ineffective negotiators will try to solve only portions of the problem.

In order to generate useful options and long-term solutions, time must be taken to gather complete information and to encourage full expression of the other party's feelings and intentions. Only when the parties have fully expressed their feelings will they feel understood. Often the other party's need to fully express and be heard is a more critical issue to him than the actual issue presented. Careful listening and encouraging opens up many possibilities for the successful negotiator.

PART THREE

YOUR MONEY AND RESOURCES

CHAPTER NINE

MONEY MANAGEMENT

*T*aking control of our money, credit, insurance privacy, and other resources is fundamental to our well-being and overall success. We must set realistic, yet aggressive, financial goals, and implement them through effective cash flow management and financial and estate planning. Maintaining good life, health, and auto insurance should be a part of everyone's risk analysis and planning. Our well-being and enjoyment of life will also depend on keeping good credit and being proactive in safeguarding our privacy and freedom from consumer fraud.

Financial Planning for The Nineties and Beyond

With career and professional success will come the need for effective money management. Much in life will depend on our financial stability—a home, a vacation, a new car, a happy lifestyle. Preparing for the 1990s and beyond will require that we all do effective financial planning, review our financial status on a regular basis and start taking the steps toward financial security.

The most important part of financial planning is getting started. "For most people, the problem is simply procrastination," says Stuart Kessler, a partner at Goldstein, Golub, Kessler & Company in New York, and chairman of the personal financial planning committee of American Institute of Certified Public Accountants.

Most people simply do not plan until a major situation occurs. In many cases, financial planing becomes crisis planning because people do not take action until a crisis is staring them in the face. But a crisis situation is usually the least practical time to make a financial decision.

Financial planning can be broken down into a few simple steps that are adaptable for anyone who is willing to work toward financial goals. If our financial plans become too elaborate and inflexible, then we may lose interest and focus. The key money and financial planning steps are:

- Setting goals through realistic financial objectives.
- Cash flow management through income and net worth analysis.
- Investment and accumulation planning through an effective balance of investment options, strategies, and risks.
- Estate planning

It is up to each of us to make our dreams come true by setting and attaining financial goals. We should review our financial status on a regular basis by determining our net worth and analyzing how our assets are allocated. We need to prepare a budget to keep track of our cash in-flows and out-flows. We should keep our financial records (such as receipts, check books, bank statements, and other important documents) organized and in a safe place. We must set adequate and achievable goals for savings and investments to provide resources for emergencies and retirement. We should do some estate planning to minimize taxes and administrative expenses, and to maximize value for our family, heirs, and other beneficiaries. We have to take steps as early as possible to lay down a financial foundation on which we can build a secure future.

Setting Financial Goals

Setting goals and objectives are critical for an effective financial plan. Start by listing and prioritizing realistic financial goals to create a working agenda. These goals should be revised periodically as conditions, needs, and other developments occur. Some common financial goals are:

- Reducing personal debt
- Obtaining financial resources to buy a home
- Providing funds for a child's college education
- Acquiring funds to start a business
- Providing adequate retirement income
- Attaining financial security and independence

Reducing Personal Debt: Debt consolidation and reduction is perhaps one of the most important financial goals. With the elimination of the tax deductibility of consumer debt, credit card and other personal debt becomes a substantial drain on a person's cash. Most individuals get trapped in the spiral of just paying off interest and not the principal balances of these accounts. This allows the interest and principal to continue the compounding process. Although savings and certificate of deposit rates have fallen tremendously, the major credit cards are still charging in excess of fifteen to eighteen percent. These high consumer interest rates can spell disaster for financial planning and security.

We need to look at ways to control our personal debt by minimizing use of credit cards and consumer credit. We should try to pay cash for most of our purchases if possible. We need to avoid a lot of impulse buying because it can wreck our financial planning. Is too much being spent on gifts? Entertainment and dining out? Vacations? Clothing? Although we should enjoy life, finding ways to curb our spending can help us in saving and investing and meeting our financial goals.

Learning to use the equity on our homes can help us manage our credit and advance our financial plans. Unlike consumer interest, home mortgage and home equity interest is tax deductible. Consider getting a home equity loan to pay off consumer loans and consolidate debt. It will likely save taxes and interest in the long run.

Obtaining Financial Resources to Buy a Home: Buying a new

home can create a financial opportunity and challenge. It is probably the largest single expenditure we will make in our lifetime. Banks and savings and loan institutions usually require ten to fifteen percent down payment and closing costs for a new home can be another ten percent. Qualified first-time home buyers may be eligible for some federal mortgages that require as little as a five percent down payment. With the deductibility of mortgage interest on a primary residence, home ownership not only has personal rewards but also financial and tax planning advantages.

Budgeting becomes important in saving for the down payment, closing costs and other expenses in buying a home. Preparing a budget helps us keep track of where our money is going. It also helps in predicting how we will spend money in the future. Budgeting is an important process in setting financial goals and making sure that we are taking the right steps toward meeting them. The budget should allow for savings to meet financial goals and objectives.

Providing Funding for a Child's College Education: Funding for a child's college education is another important financial goal. Today a college education is likely to cost over $20,000 a year for a private school and $10,000 a year for a public school. These costs are projected to increase significantly over the forthcoming years. The earlier a person starts to save for college, the easier it will be to accumulate the required funds.

Use the college cost worksheet below to calculate the costs of a college education for the kids and the required annual savings:

1. Estimating the Cost of College.
   Enter the name and age of the child in the space provided on the worksheet below. In the next space, enter the estimated annual cost for tuition, fees, and room and board at the institution he or she is likely to attend.

   Next, look up the Estimated Future Cost Factor (based on an average annual increase of six percent as projected

by many college planning experts) on the chart below.
Multiply the current college cost by the estimated future
cost factor. This is the estimate of the total four-year future
cost for the child's college education.

Name & Age of Child	Current Annual College Cost $	Estimated Future Cost Factor ×	Total College Costs in Future Dollars = $

2. What Will Need to Be Saved.

Multiply the Total College Costs in Future Dollars from Step
1 above times the Required Savings Factor below. This is
an estimate of the annual savings required to accumulate
enough money for the children's college education.

Age of Child	Estimated Future Cost Factor	Required Savings Factor*
1	11.780	0.025
2	11.113	0.027
3	10.484	0.031
4	9.891	0.034
5	9.331	0.038
6	8.803	0.043
7	8.304	0.049
8	7.834	0.056
9	7.391	0.064
10	6.972	0.074
11	6.578	0.087
12	6.205	0.104
13	5.854	0.126
14	5.523	0.158
15	5.210	0.205
16	5.915	0.285

| 17 | 4.637 | 0.445 |
| 18 | 4.375 | 0.926 |

* This factor assumes a hypothetical average rate of return of eight percent.

Encourage other family members to contribute to a child's college fund at gift time. Structuring the monies as "uniform gift to minors account" allows some favorable tax treatment. These accounts are set up where the custodian is the parent for the child's account. The accounts are taxed at the parent's tax rate for the first fourteen years. When the child turns age fourteen the account is taxed at the child's tax rate. It is beneficial to get the child involved in saving some of the money towards his or her college education. This creates a partnership in saving and helps instill financial responsibility in our children.

Acquiring Funds to Start a Business: Adequate funding is important to starting a business. Most experts recommend that a person have saved a year's salary and operating expenses before pursuing his own business. He should also arrange a line of credit with a bank or other financial institution. Refer to chapter five for additional information on achieving the goal of business ownership.

Providing Adequate Retirement Income: Although Social Security provides some basic benefits, our financial independence during retirement will likely come from our pensions, savings, investments, and other financial resources. This means that now more than ever we will be responsible for providing for our own retirement. This means using our employer-sponsored 401(k) savings to maximize our financial benefits. We should try to contribute as much money as possible to our 401(k) plan. The earnings that we save are usually tax-deferred, and many employers match the 401(k) contribution. Also, a person can typically borrow money from his 401(k) at below market interest rates and the interest is tax-deferred income to him. We can advantageously use our 401(k) loans to pay off credit cards and other consumer debts.

Use the retirement planning chart below to set financial goals for retirement:

Your Retirement Needs

1. Annual income needed when you retire
    (80% of pre-retirement income).

    $ _____

2. Probable Social Security and pension benefits.
    Refer to the "Projected annual Social Security
    benefits" chart below. Add to that figure what
    your employee benefits counselor estimated
    your annual pension will be in today's dollars.

    $ _____

3. Annual retirement income needed from
    investments (line 1 minus line 2).

    $ _____

4. Amount you must save before retirement
    (line 3 times factor A below).

    $ _____

5. Amount you have saved already, including IRAs,
    corporate savings plans and other investments.

    $ _____

6. Projected value of your current retirement savings
    at the time you retire (line 5 times factor B).

    $ _____

7. Amount of retirement capital still needed
    (line 4 minus line 6).

    $ _____

8. Annual savings needed to reach your goal
    (line 7 times factor C).

    $ _____

9. Total you should save each year (line 8 minus
    annual employer contributions to savings plan).

    $ _____

Projected Annual Social Security Benefits

Worker's current age		Worker's Earnings in 1993			
		$30,000	$40,000	$50,000	$60,000+
45	Worker	$13,908	$15,624	$17,232	$17,892
	Worker with spouse	20,856	23,436	25,848	26,832
55	Worker	$12,624	$13,308	$14,772	$15,096
	Worker with spouse	18,936	20,700	22,152	22,644
65	Worker	$11,724	$12,456	$12,972	$13,056
	Worker with spouse	17,580	18,684	19,452	19,584

Source: Social Security Administration, 1992

Age at Retirement	55	56	57	58	59	60	61	62	63	64	65	66	67
Factor A	23.3	22.9	22.6	22.2	21.8	21.4	21.0	20.5	20.1	19.6	19.2	18.7	18.2

Year to Retirement	5	7	9	11	13	15	20	25	30
Factor B	1.15	1.22	1.29	1.36	1.44	1.53	1.76	2.02	2.33
Factor C	0.188	0.131	0.099	0.079	0.065	0.054	0.038	0.028	0.022

The factors listed above assume a hypothetical 8% total return and a 5% rate of inflation.

Attaining Financial Security and Independence: The definition of financial security will be different for each of us. Our goal of financial security may be creating a portfolio of $500,000 in marketable securities which will allow us to live off the interest and dividends. It may be having a cushion of six months salary to protect us in case of unemployment or an emergency.

Whatever our idea of financial security and independence, a good financial planner can be helpful in analyzing our finances and recommending how to improve our financial situation. They can assist in preparing a financial plan based on our personal history and financial goals. Before selecting a financial planner be sure to investigate his or her background and experience.

For further information on financial planners contact the following organizations:

National Association of Personal Financial Advisors
1130 Lake Cook Road, Suite 105
Buffalo Grove, Illinois 60089
1-800-366-2732

Institute of Certified Financial Planners
7600 E. Eastman Avenue, Suite 301
Denver, Colorado 80231
(303) 751-7600

International Association for Financial Planning
2 Concourse Parkway, Suite 800
Atlanta, Georgia 30328
(404) 395-1605

Securities and Exchange Commission
Office of Filings, Information, and Consumer Services
450 5th Street, N.W.
Washington, D.C. 20549
(202) 272-5624

A successful strategy for maximizing our financial security should comprise 1) controlling our personal debt and expenditures; 2) saving regularly; 3) taking full advantage of tax-deferred and tax-free income plans; and 4) maintaining a diversified and risk-balanced investment portfolio.

Cash Flow Management

Managing our disposable income is critical in allowing us to reach our financial goals and objectives. A starting point is to establish a workable budget using the cash flow worksheet below. First we list all sources of our income, such as salary and other payments we receive. Next, we should list all of our expenses and expenditures. It is important to itemize all variable and fixed costs. Normally, the fixed costs like mortgage, rent, and taxes are easy to identify. But variable costs like entertainment, meals, and hobbies might be harder to quantify. A helpful exercise is to make journal entries on all cash expenditures on a daily and weekly basis. Once all the major categories are identified it is critical to establish spending guidelines for all areas. Subtracting expenses from income gives the disposable income to use for savings and investments.

Cash Flow Worksheet

		PER MONTH
Your income:	Wages, salary, and commissions	$ _____
	Dividends, interest, and capital gains	_____
	Annuities, pensions and Social Security	_____
	Death benefits from estate	_____
	Income on real property	_____
	Other	_____
	Total Income	_____
Your Expenses:	Taxes	_____
	Mortgage/Rent	_____
	Medical expenses	_____
	Utilities	_____
	Telephone	_____
	Car	_____
	Clothing	_____
	Childcare	_____
	Tuition or education expenses	_____
	Insurance premiums	_____
	Maintenance of home	_____
	Maintenance of car	_____
	Hobbies	_____
	Entertainment	_____
	Vacations	_____

Memberships/Professional fees   _____
Gifts and donations   _____
Loans, credit cards   _____
Other   _____
    Total Expenses   _____
Total Income   _____
(minus) Total Expenses   _____
Total Available for Savings/Investments   _____

Determining our net worth periodically lets us know where we are financially. Net worth is calculated by totalling all of the assets and subtracting all of the debts and other liabilities. We can start with the preparation of a net worth statement by listing all of our assets and their value. This should include cash, checking, and savings accounts, certificates of deposits, stock, bonds, IRA accounts, life insurance cash values, real estate, automobiles, and personal property. Next, we list all of our liabilities, including mortgages, personal loans, credit cards, taxes, and any other debts. The sum of our assets minus our liabilities will tell us how much we are worth.

Use the worksheet below to calculate your net worth:

Net Worth Worksheet

LIQUID ASSETS	CURRENT VALUE		LIABILITIES
Checking accounts	_____	Credit card balances	_____
Savings accounts	_____		
Money market funds	_____	Education loans	_____
Cash value of line insurance	_____		
Other liquid assets	_____		_____
	_____	Car loans	_____
	_____	Personal installment loans	_____
Total liquid assets	_____	Other loans	_____

149

INVESTMENT ASSETS

Mutual funds	_____		
Stocks	_____	Mortgage	_____
Bonds	_____		_____
Certificates of deposit	_____	Other liabilities	_____

RETIREMENT PLANS

IRA	_____		_____
401(k) plan	_____		_____
Company pension	_____		_____
Other retirement	_____		_____
plan(s)	_____	Total liabilities	_____
Other investment assets	_____		
Total investment assets	_____		

PERSONAL ASSETS

Residence	_____	Total assets	_____
Vacation property	_____		
Jewelry/art/antiques	_____	Minus total liabilities	_____
	_____	Your Personal Net	
Total personal assets	_____	Worth	_____
Total assets	_____		

Selecting a Financial Institution

Here are some tips from the U.S. Office of Consumer Affairs for choosing a financial institution for checking, saving and other financial needs.

Finding the right bank, savings and loan, or credit union means figuring out our own needs first. Answering the following questions should help you identify your "banking personality" and make choosing a financial institution a bit easier.

• What is your goal in establishing a banking relationship?

Answers might include "to save money," "to have a checking account," "to get a loan," or all of the above.

* How much money can you keep on deposit each month and how many checks will you write? Knowing this will help you judge how complex or simple an account you need.

* Will you be buying a home or car or making another large purchase in the near future? If so, you'll want to find out about the types of loans offered by the institutions you are considering.

* If you hope to save for a big expense or toward your child's (or your own) future education, you'll also want to find out how many different savings programs are offered.

* What time of day do you prefer to do your banking? Do you like the convenience of automated teller machines (ATMs) or do you prefer to deal with live tellers? Answering these two questions will help you determine if you'd be happier at a financial institution with regular, evening or weekend hours, or one with a wide network of ATMs.

* What does the financial institution charge for services like cashier's checks, safe deposit boxes and stop payment orders? Is there a charge for using an automated teller machine? Is there a monthly service charge, or must you maintain a minimum balance in your account to avoid a charge?

After answering the above questions, we should now be ready to narrow our options to specific financial institutions. We should phone or visit several near our homes or offices because they are likely to be the most convenient. We can take our answers to the above questions with us and find out which accounts and services are most likely to match our needs. We can then compare fees and service charges, as well as deposit and loan interest rates.

Price might not be the most important factor in our "banking personality," so we also should take a minute to think about how comfortable we feel at each institution. For example, are questions answered quickly and accurately? Do customer service personnel offer helpful suggestions?

Remember, we can choose more than one financial institution to provide us with different banking services.

Before making a final choice, make sure the institutions being considered are federally insured. This means deposits will be protected up to $100,000.

Investment Planning

There are a myriad of savings and investment vehicles available for both short-term and long-term financial goals. These include everything from the simple savings account with banks, credit unions, and savings and loans associations to U.S. Government securities, corporate and municipal bonds, mutual funds, annuities, stocks, real estate, and commodities. An effective investment strategy is to balance risks, yield, taxes, inflation, and liquidity with the best mix of investment channels.

The best investment strategy should be one of prudent risk-taking. With most investments, the greater risks usually provide the potential for a greater return. However, our level of risk taking typically changes over our various life cycles. At a younger age we can afford to take greater risk as we strive to build up our investment assets. When we approach retirement, our risk factor should decline as we focus on minimizing losses and preserving asset value. Financial planners have various investing guidelines depending on our age and investment horizons. One example is—subtract age from one hundred and that number could represent the percentage of assets that should be in stock. However, to help reduce overall risk of loss, an investment portfolio should always be diversified into a variety of investment vehicles.

The U.S. Government offers securities which are very safe with guaranteed rates of return. Treasury bills are issued for periods of thirteen, twenty-six, or fifty-two weeks and are redeemable for the face amount. The purchaser pays a discounted amount, and the yield over the time period of the bills is the difference between the face value and the discounted price. Treasury bills can be purchased directly from local Federal Reserve Bank without paying any fees or through an intermediary bank or broker.

The U.S. Treasury also offers EE and Series HH savings bonds. EE bonds mature in twelve years and guarantee a minimum six percent rate. If held for five years or longer we will typically earn a competitive market-based rate on EE bonds. We can purchase EE bonds at a discounted price and receive the face value of the bonds on maturity. The interest earned on EE bonds is exempt from state and local taxes and we pay no federal taxes on the interest income until we cash in the bonds. Series HH bonds are also exempt from state and local taxes and earn six percent annual interest which is paid semi-annually. The EE and HH savings bonds are very safe investments and can usually be purchased through banks and other financial institutions, or through employers by payroll deduction.

Municipal bonds are another relatively safe investment vehicle. Although their yields are usually lower than most riskier investments, the interest earned is typically exempt from federal, state, and local taxes. Municipal bonds can be a useful investment medium if the investor is in a high tax bracket.

Corporate bonds are an additional investment medium which can offer attractive yields at relatively low to medium risks, depending on the financial health of the issuing company and its bond rating. Bonds with the highest grade are rated as "AAA," and these typically offer a lower yield than the lower grade bonds. Corporate bonds are usually issued from one to thirty years and are redeemable for the face value at maturity. The bonds are purchased at a discounted price which fluctuates according to market conditions.

Most people are probably already familiar with the savings plans offered by their banks, such as the traditional passbook savings account. Banks also offer certificates of deposit with varying maturity periods and interest rates. There are usually penalties for early withdrawal of funds from certificates of deposit. Money market accounts are also available at most banks and generally earn a higher yield than passbook savings accounts. The money market accounts may provide check-writing and other privileges, and may be subject to minimum balance requirements and administrative fees. Accounts with federally insured banks and credit unions are insured up to $100,000 per depositor.

Annuities from insurance companies or other financial establishments are investment vehicles which guarantee a fixed income for life or a specified number of years. If someone wants a guaranteed income without having to worry about managing assets to attain it, then he should consider purchasing an annuity. The interest is usually tax-deferred until withdrawals are made. Annuities are only as good as the company issuing them, so be sure to investigate the financial health of the company before purchasing an annuity.

Riskier investments include equity or ownership vehicles such as stocks, mutual funds, commodities, and real estate. When we purchase stock, we are buying part ownership in a company. The value of stock will go up and down depending on the financial performance of the company and other economic conditions. The stock may also pay dividends determined by company profits. Regular ownership in a company is evidenced by common stock which has no guaranteed rate of return; in fact, the return can be negative. Preferred stock usually offer a specified dividend rate and is paid off before common stock if the company dissolves.

Historically, stocks have outperformed most other financial assets such as bonds, money markets, and metals. Over a twenty-year horizon a stock portfolio, on average, will likely generate the most growth and help keep assets constant with inflation.

Mutual funds are a mechanism by which we can pool our assets with other investors for investing in a variety of vehicles. Some mutual funds can be speculative and extremely risky and others can be conservative depending on how the fund makes investments. It is very important that a fund's historical performance and financial stability be evaluated before investing in mutual funds.

Real estate and commodities are purely speculative investments and involve a lot of risk. With these investments a person is gambling on the future value of assets such as real property, precious metals, foreign currencies, and feed stocks. Always obtain professional advice before investing in high risk ventures.

Effective Estate Planning

Estate planning plays an important function in managing our financial resources. Two-thirds of high net worth individuals fail to understand and take advantage of laws and procedures regarding transferring wealth to someone else. Without proper planning we may inadvertently allocate an unnecessarily large portion of our estate to pay taxes and expenses. With planning, we can determine the value of our estate and make decisions while we are alive that will preserve it for our heirs later. Through the use of various tools of estate planning, like charitable trusts, living trusts, and life insurance we may be able to avoid some tremendous costs to our estate.

An estate plan is normally used to preserve the estate today and minimize the cost associated with dividing and transferring the value to heirs later. The plan should also consider ways to accomplish other goals we have for assets that we have accumulated during our lifetime. If our estate plan costs us more than it saves, it is an ineffective plan.

The key to estate planning is establishing goals. Prior to deciding on the use of estate planning devices such as a will or various trusts, each of us should decide what we would like to accomplish with our estate. Is preservation for our heirs important? Would we like to maximize the value to us now or our heirs later? Are we willing to sacrifice a portion of what we have today to leave more for others later? Would we consider giving assets to charity? Don't get lost in the details on the type of trusts or wills needed because these are merely tools to be used to accomplish the objectives. Rather than thinking about the how, and what kind of will or trust, think of the why. We should let the professionals worry about how to put our wishes into proper form. We need to tell our estate planner or attorney what we want accomplished so they can help us accomplish our goals.

There are two provisions in the tax law that determine the amount that may be passed to heirs without incurring estate taxes. The first is that when an estate is left to a surviving spouse, regardless of size, there is no estate tax due. The amount that may be passed to a spouse at death is unlimited. This is the unlimited marital deduction.

The second provision involves the United Credit which pertains to amounts passed to other heirs. Currently, the tax law allows for a credit of $192,800 against estate taxes due. This credit is equivalent to the tax due on $600,000 of assets. Therefore if we die with an estate of $600,000 or less there would be no estate taxes due, in most cases. A married couple may leave $1,200,000 to heirs since they are entitled to two unified credits.

Note that in many cases one of the unified credits is lost at the death of the first spouse unless the couple take steps necessary to preserve that credit. Remember, as long as money passes to one spouse there are no estate taxes because of the unlimited marital deduction. But, upon the death of the second, taxes will be due on any amount over $600,000. One basic element of estate planning for married couples should be preserving both unified credits. Working with a good estate planner can help us maximize benefits under the tax laws.

Estate Planning Devices

A will and trust arrangement can be used as effective estate planning devices. A will is a set of final instructions showing how we would like our property distributed. Although none of us like to think of our own demise and the need for a will, it is a necessary document if we have assets and would like to have these distributed according to our wishes. In the absence of a will, court proceedings may be necessary to determine how our estate should be distributed. Thus, a will should be a part of any estate plan.

A revocable living trust is a legal arrangement to hold property during one's life for the benefit of others at one's death. It may be used jointly with a will. The revocable living trust may be changed at anytime by the grantor (the person who sets up the trust). Assets continue under the control of the grantor. This type of trust is normally set up to avoid the time and costs of probate.

An irrevocable trust is another arrangement for holding property and can be useful in estate planning. The irrevocable trust, once established, generally can not be changed and the grantor gives up control over assets transferred to the trust.

Another estate planning device is the charitable remainder trust which allows a person to give assets to a charity without giving up income from the assets during his lifetime. Assets are placed in trust for the benefit of a charity at the death of the grantor. During the grantor's lifetime the trust will pay an income stream to the grantor. The grantor will normally receive an income tax deduction when assets are placed into the trust. The amount of the income tax deduction is calculated using IRS guidelines. This type of trust is used to provide income today. It is particularly useful when a sale of highly appreciated assets are involved.

Life insurance can be used as an effective estate planning device to transfer the value of assets to heirs. Since life insurance usually avoids probate and administrative expenses, it is an excellent way to transfer assets.

Gifting and joint ownership arrangements may also be used as part of an overall estate plan. Each one has its advantages and disadvantages. Prior to using a gifting or joint ownership arrangement we need to make sure we fully understand that this also means giving up control over our assets. We can make gifts to an unlimited number of people or organizations without paying federal gift taxes, provided that these gifts do not exceed $10,000

($20,000 for married couples) per person each year. No taxes are paid on gifts of any amount between spouses.

Because tax and estate laws are constantly changing, people should always seek the advice of a knowledgeable attorney or estate planner before making gift and estate planning decisions.

Setting Up Your Estate Plan

There is cost involved in setting up an estate plan. However, by investing money and time today, we may be saving our heirs not only thousands of dollars but also legal and emotional distress later.

Here are steps we can follow in setting up an estate plan:

- Determine the current value of the estate. Include all assets plus the death benefit from any life insurance policies. Include cash value of policies that are owned even if the owner is not the insured.
- Set goals. What would we like to accomplish with our assets? Do we want to preserve the full value for relatives, charity, or others? Any specific bequests (the family heirloom to our daughter)? Any special needs that should be addressed, like providing for the care of a minor or handicapped heir?
- Evaluate our present situation. What costs would be incurred if our estate were settled today, and how would assets be distributed to heirs? Do we have a current will? Does it reflect our true wishes? We need to make an itemized list of costs for settling our estate. Include funeral expenses, estate taxes, income taxes, probate and legal fees, and payment of creditors. Will there be a cash shortage in settling the estate? If so, it may be necessary to sell assets to cover the shortage. Oftentimes a forced sale of assets can result in diminished market value. This is the "before" picture. A financial analysis done by a financial planner should accomplish the above. The

analysis should also point out the dollars that may be saved by making changes in our present situation.

- Compare the "before" picture with goals. Are changes desirable? Together with an estate planning professional determine what changes need to be made to accomplish these goals.
- Determine the cost that would be incurred to make changes to the "before" picture.
- Evaluate the "after" picture. How will circumstances differ when changes are in place? What problems will an estate plan solve? Will it eliminate cash shortages? Will there be a change in the value of the estate to heirs? Will asset distribution be correct? Is there a benefit today?
- Compare costs versus benefits and make a decision on the appropriate course of action. Develop an action plan to complete all necessary steps. Include a time frame to get things done.
- Implement the plan. Otherwise, the best laid plans do not accomplish a thing. If we do not follow through and actually implement the plan, we have wasted time and money.
- Review annually. Since everything changes, laws, value of our estate, our personal preferences, etc. we should establish a time for review of our plan at least once a year.

SMART MANEUVERS

CHAPTER TEN

MAINTAINING GOOD INSURANCE

Is insurance really necessary? There is life insurance, auto insurance, home insurance, medical insurance, flood insurance, mortgage insurance, and more. How much of this do we really need?

From a financial perspective insurance serves a necessary function. Few of us are prepared financially to handle the risks of a catastrophic loss. If an unexpected loss would cause financial problems for us, our dependents, our business, or others, then insurance might be prudent to cover the potential loss. Also, if our debts exceed our available assets we should consider life insurance or debt insurance to cover the shortage to avoid creating a financial burden for our family or our business. Our insurance requirements should be reviewed regularly to assure that we are protected against possible unacceptable financial losses.

Do You Need Insurance?

Insurance is a necessity to guard against losses and liabilities. It is basically a contract between us and an insurance company. This contract is typically referred to as an insurance policy. The insurance company usually agrees to pay a "benefit" upon the occurrence of a certain event to a designated "beneficiary" in exchange for a "premium." The policy owner may typically name the insured person, place, or event and the beneficiary. The policy usually has a time component, benefits, a premium, and may include other terms governing the relationship between us and the insurance company. The policy, such as a life insurance policy, may include savings, dividends, and special provisions for loans, along with riders covering special circumstances.

With any insurance, the risk of a devastating financial loss is passed off to an insurance company that has the resources to cover the loss. When considering insurance we should be certain the company we choose has the financial assets necessary to cover expected losses. We need to be sure the insurance company is likely to be around with the dollars necessary if we need them. Don't buy insurance from a company that does not have a good reputation and a high rating by BEST, Standard & Poor's, or Moody's agencies.

Every insurance policy has premiums—the amount we submit to the insurance company in exchange for the coverage we receive. But premiums vary with the type and amount of insurance and other factors. Some policies, such as whole life insurance, have cash value after a period of time; meaning that they are a form of investment or savings which allows us to get a return over time for some of our premium payments.

Like most financial products, insurance policies cover a wide range. Even among the life insurance policies there are offered term, whole life, single premium life, joint life, second to die, universal, and variable life, to name a few. What should we know about insurance in order to make an intelligent choice? Do we need to understand every facet of every available policy? With a basic understanding of the way insurance works and our own financial needs, we will be in a good position to make an intelligent selection.

Reviewing Your Life Insurance Needs

Life insurance is designed to protect us, our families or our businesses from the loss resulting from our death, or the death of someone else. If we are a major source of income for our families, we are likely to need some form of life insurance. The same applies to our spouses.

There is a wide range of products available when choosing life insurance. Insurance companies are combining investment options and flexibility to create life insurance and investment products for specific groups. With this variety, we should be able to find life insurance that fits our needs and makes sense for each of our financial situations.

From a financial perspective, when we buy a life insurance policy we commit ourselves to a small regular financial loss in the form of insurance premiums in exchange for coverage in the event of an unexpected death, which could be accompanied by a much larger financial loss. The policy may offer various incentives to soften or lower the financial cost. One key incentive may be a savings or dividend component. For these reasons people should stop thinking about premiums only as a cost of insurance. Premiums can also be an investment and savings mechanism.

The main reason for having life insurance is usually for the death benefit. Before making a decision on life insurance we should determine what size death benefit is needed to cover all the financial requirements that would result from a premature death.

For our dependents the value of life insurance is obvious— we can create an "instant estate" which provides for a surviving spouse and children to the extent that we can afford and desire to do so. When considering life insurance take some time to do the arithmetic. What sort of financial stability would we want to provide for our families or other beneficiaries? What type of financial stability do we and our spouses want to provide each other in the event of a death. We need to consider things like existing debts, final expenses, and inflation. Do we want to provide for college for children? What about other unexpected expenses?

After selecting the right death benefit, we should look at the other benefits that may be available from our policies. As with any contract we must make sure we are getting what we want and make sure we understand our obligations for premium payments;

how much and when due. Find out if payments can be skipped and coverage still retained? How many years do premiums continue? Get an understanding of other benefits that may be acquired and what these will cost.

For the best results in selecting life insurance coverage, we should always follow these basic steps:

- Compute the amount of insurance needed. What amount of financial loss would we like to cover in the event of a premature death? What amount of financial resources have we accumulated to cover the loss?
- Determine the type of policy desired. Do we want cash value or term? How many years will we need coverage? Do we have a long term savings need? Is tax deferral on savings important?
- Select a competent and trustworthy insurance agent. Purchase life insurance from a reputable insurance company.
- Compare various insurance companies, policy options, and costs.
- Read our life insurance policies and make sure that we understand our coverage, exclusions, and other provisions.
- Let our families and beneficiaries know about our life insurance policies and where we keep them.
- Review our life insurance needs and our insurance policies at least annually. Is the beneficiary correct? Should the amount of insurance be increased or decreased? Should we invest additional cash in a policy or take some of the cash value? Does our insurance fit our estate planning needs?

What Type of Life Insurance?

Basically, there are two types of life insurance, term and cash value (commonly referred to as whole life). Insurance companies vary these term and cash value policies and mix the two in single policies to satisfy market demands. When considering the products on the life insurance market be aware that life insurance products are tailored to meet specific needs and objectives. If we do not have the time to thoroughly review the market, we should get a competent, trusted agent who will be concerned about our insurance needs and our financial situations. We should try to find an agent who has knowledge of a wide range of products so that he or she will make the best recommendations for our particular circumstances.

A term insurance policy provides life insurance for a specified period of time, such as one year, five years, twenty years, or up to a certain age. In some cases there may be provisions for renewal, but premiums will likely increase upon renewal because we are older. Term policies are usually "bare bones" policies with few extras. If we will need life insurance for a limited period of time and have limited discretionary income, term life insurance may be our best buy. It may be the only way we can afford the coverage we need at this point. If we can afford more and have a long term need for life insurance, perhaps something other than term may be better.

Generally, if we will need life insurance for more than ten years, it may be to our advantage to consider cash value policies that offer a savings or investment element. Most term policies expire without ever paying any death benefits. If our insurance needs will extend well into the future, we should be aware of the escalating cost of our term policies. We may reach the point in our older years when the cost of term insurance is out of our reach. Term insurance may be less expensive in the short term, but not in the long term. If someone plans to leave a sizeable estate to heirs through life insurance, then term policies typically will not be the best choice.

One of the disadvantages of term policies is the termination date. After a specific period of time the term policy will end with no cash value. There are policies available that are guaranteed renewable or that may offer the right to convert the term policy to a cash value policy. But, in most cases term policies will expire with no provisions for renewal or conversion. If our circumstances change or we become uninsurable because of health during the period that we are covered by a term policy, we may be unable to find life insurance when we need it most.

The advantages of term life insurance is its simplicity and low cost, in early years. The disadvantages are its termination date, increasing premiums, and lack of cash value and limited tax advantages.

Cash value life insurance can be used to describe all the other life insurance, except term insurance. The common feature of cash value insurance policies it that they combine an element of insurance with an investment or savings account. There may be good financial reasons why we would want to choose cash value insurance, particularly if we have a long term need for life insurance. As with most long term investments there may be a longer period of time before we see a good payoff from a cash value life insurance policy. If we bail out early, we may lose money. However, if our cash value insurance is properly selected to suit our particular financial circumstances, the return can be attractive in the long run.

Cash value life insurance has basically two components—the cost component and the savings/investment component. The cost component is the portion of our premium that actually pays for our death benefit coverage. Since cash value policies increase in value as we pay premiums, not all of the premium is used to cover the death benefit. The charge for the death benefit is less than the amount of our premiums which results in a balance (cash accumulation) in our accounts which accumulates over time. As our cash accumulates it earns a return which also accumulates in our accounts.

The cash value in our policies is generally available through loans or surrender of the policy even before the death benefit is payable. Remember that a key advantage gained for earnings on life insurance cash account is its tax-deferred status. If the value in the cash account does not exceed the amount paid in premiums, taxes on the earnings may be avoided because these are viewed as a return of premiums. Cash value insurance policies will typically provide us with several methods for withdrawing our dollars. The cash value in our insurance policy is usually available quickly and provides us with a very liquid asset.

There are typically three ways to get money from our cash value policies. We may borrow against the cash value of the policy, usually at some interest rate which is below the market rate. If we should die before the loan is repaid, the amount owed plus any interest will be subtracted from the death benefits which will be paid to our beneficiaries. We may also surrender the policy and the insurance company will pay us the cash value. With surrenders there may be a surrender charge, particularly in the early years of a policy. We need to make sure that we understand any surrender charges, how we can avoid them; and when surrender charges will not apply. Lastly, we can typically use the cash value of our policies to buy an annuity that provides a guaranteed monthly income for life.

Whole life is one of the most common cash value policies. Whole life policies have a guaranteed death benefit, guaranteed interest rate, and guaranteed premium over the life of the policy. Generally whole life policies pay a lower rate of interest than other cash value policies. Whole life policies are usually designed to have the cash value equal to the death benefit when the insured reaches age one hundred. If there is a short term insurance need or if insurance needs are likely to change, a whole life policy may not be best.

The advantages of whole life are its fixed death benefit, fixed premium, lifetime coverage, tax advantages, and cash value. Its disadvantages are its relative inflexibility, low rate of return, and higher initial cost.

Using Life Insurance to Meet Financial Goals

Life insurance policies can be used effectively to accumulate cash for long term goals. For example, insurance needs may be coupled with a long term savings need, such as funding retirement or providing an education fund for children. A cash value policy offers the best opportunities through life insurance to reach some of our long range financial goals.

Remember the variety of options that may be available by having a large cash value accumulate within our life insurance policies: 1) We can purchase an annuity; 2) We can borrow against the total cash value; 3) We may surrender the policy for the full cash value; 4) We can use the policy as a gift or transfer wealth to our heirs. Life insurance can also be used as a means for paying for estate taxes, medical expenses, funeral expenses, and other needs.

The first step in utilizing life insurance effectively is to determine our financial needs and the amount of insurance necessary to cover them. Some financial advisors recommend that we should have life insurance equal to five times each of our total annual earnings. Thus, if our annual income is $50,000, life insurance in the amount of $250,000 is suggested.

However, this general rule may not apply to everyone, because of special circumstances and financial needs. For example, we may want to provide financial stability for our families for five years, pay off our mortgages, and educate our children. If annual income is $50,000, mortgage on the home is $160,000, and cost of education for our children is $60,000, life insurance needs can be calculated as follows:

Five year income	$250,000
Mortgage	160,000
Education	60,000
Total need	$470,000

Less:

Current coverage and investment	$10,000
Savings for education	10,000
Employer paid insurance	100,000

Total $120,000

Life Insurance need $350,000

We should take time to figure our financial needs, including income needs, mortgage, final expenses, education costs, and other debts. We need to make sure we allow for inflation and sub-tract present assets that might be used. We can make wise life insurance decisions if we go through a comprehensive review of our responsibilities, financial requirements, and resources. People should examine their life insurance needs periodically to take into account changes in family circumstances, living arrangements, and other variables.

We should explain our life insurance coverage to our families and beneficiaries. We should give them our agent's name and address and a photocopy of our policies. Our beneficiaries should also know where we keep our life insurance policies, because upon our death they will need to send them to our insurance companies along with a copy of the death certificate to get paid.

One of the real advantages to investing in life insurance is the favorable tax treatment of distributions from insurance policies. If we are careful about the way we take distributions we may be able to receive our life insurance earnings effectively tax-free. Return of premiums generally is not taxed. Loans against cash values may also avoid taxes. With planning we can effectively withdraw most of the value of our policies through loans and surrenders and avoid any income taxes.

An additional advantage for estate planning purposes may be the death benefit. The death benefit will be paid to our bene-ficiaries and generally will not be subject to estate or income taxes.

Although there are a number of methods to obtain the cash value from our life insurance, we should pay careful attention to how we fund the policy and how we take the cash. We should consult our insurance agent or tax advisor to review our specific case and how to comply with IRS regulations. Otherwise, we may be taxed on distributions from our policies first as a return of earnings and may face other tax penalties.

Keeping Good Health Insurance

A major illness or disability can be financially devastating if we don't have adequate health insurance. The problem of access to health care in America has generated a great deal of public attention over the past few years. Over forty million Americans lack health insurance. One-third of the U.S. population with incomes below the poverty level don't even qualify for Medicaid—a joint federal-state program providing health care for the poor. While nearly ninety-eight percent of older Americans are enrolled in Medicare—a federal health insurance program for people age sixty-five and older—most remain unprotected against the catastrophic cost of long-term care and medication.

Although a national health insurance program is under consideration, each of us must ultimately make sure that health care financing is provided for us and our families. We must review our needs for medical insurance coverage and compare the various options. We need to understand what types of coverage we can obtain through employer group insurance, health maintenance organizations, and other private health insurance— as well as Medicaid, Medicare, Veterans Administration and other government-sponsored health insurance programs.

Many employers provide group health insurance for their employees. Some plans also offer spousal and family benefits. Some associations and organizations offer similar group health insurance to its members. These group health plans usually pay eighty percent or more of most major medical and hospital costs. There is typically an annual deductible in the range of about $1,000–$3,000. Our employer group health insurance is provided at little or no cost to us in many cases. In other cases, it is still substantially cheaper than buying private health insurance on our own, and the costs usually are payroll-deducted.

Upon our termination or retirement, we may be able to

convert our employer group insurance coverage into a suitable private health insurance policy. Under federal law we have the option to continue our employer-sponsored health insurance for eighteen months or more if we are terminated. In such a case, we should carefully compare the benefits and costs of our plans with other policies. If switching to another policy, be sure to continue coverage under the old policy long enough to cover any waiting periods the new policy may have. A waiting period is the time between the date when a person becomes insured and the date when the policy will pay benefits for a pre-existing condition or certain other specified illnesses.

None of us should drop our policies with our former employers without adequate advice. If the premium is paid by our former employers, or even if a small amount is paid by us, it is sometimes wise to retain the policy and buy a minimum benefit supplemental policy for complete coverage. We can contact our employer's personnel office for additional information.

The following suggestions will help us in making the best private health insurance decision for ourselves:

- Comparison shop with respect to coverage and cost. Make a chart that will show how the different plans compare with respect to such items as deductibles, coinsurance, and prescription drugs.
- Buy only the amount of insurance reasonably needed.
- Look at whether the policy pays a set dollar amount or a percentage of the cost of care. Keep in mind that inflation causes policies with fixed dollar amounts to lose relative value over time.
- Look at how long the coverage will last.
- Check for waiting periods, pre-existing conditions, exclusions, and noncovered medical services, such as treatment of mental illness, alcoholism, or drug addiction.
- Find out how much hospital care, nursing home care, and home health care cost in the area, in order to determine if policy coverage will be adequate.

- Check on the right to renew the policy. Automatic renewal policies offer the best protection.
- Beware of illegal insurance sales practices! We should not believe anyone who tells us that he or she is from the government and tries to sell us insurance. Medicare supplement policies are not sold or serviced by the Medicare program or any other state or federal government agency. Further, it is illegal for any insurance company or agent to knowingly sell us a policy that duplicates Medicare coverage or our private health plan. Insurance companies or agents that violate this law are subject to federal penalties. A person should call his state insurance department or call the U.S. Department of Health and Human Services at 1-800-638-6833 if he thinks he has been a victim of an illegal insurance sales practice.
- Don't be pressured by a salesperson. Take the time needed to make an informed decision.
- Upon receiving the policy, do not delay reading it. Make sure that it provides the coverage that was ordered.

HMOs as a Health Care Alternative

Under many health care plans, people have the option of signing up for a Health Maintenance Organization (HMO). HMOs are health care delivery systems that provide health care in exchange for a fixed, monthly fee. Under these plans, beneficiaries typically receive all covered hospital and medical insurance benefits through the plan. The cost of this type of plan is known in advance and is generally limited to the fixed monthly premiums and minimal copayments.

At no extra cost, some HMOs provide services beyond what regular health insurance covers. Examples of such services include prescription drugs and hearing aids. However, most HMOs have limits on care that people should be aware of before enrolling.

There are certain advantages to joining an HMO:
- In an HMO, we generally pay a monthly fee, which entitles

us to a wide range of medical services. In exchange for the fee, we will not be charged substantial additional costs for our medical care. People who participate in HMOs tend to use their service more frequently and at earlier stages of illness.

* The HMO may also absorb any applicable deductibles or coinsurance and provide additional benefits beyond regular services.
* HMOs tend to emphasize preventive health care, an attractive benefit for many people.

There are also certain disadvantages of joining an HMO:

* The main disadvantage is that we may not able to choose our own doctors and hospital. In general, we must obtain all our health care services through the HMO. In many cases, however, this is not a real problem because many HMOs have excellent doctors and maintain first rate health care facilities.
* To be eligible for HMO coverage, we may be required to live in the HMO's geographical area for a certain period of time. Therefore, if we travel a great deal, an HMO may not be a viable option for us.
* HMOs do not cover every possible health problem. For example, long-term care, as well as routine dental care, eyeglasses, and hearing aids are generally not covered.

Lowering Your Auto Insurance Costs

With the increasing number of cars on the road, having good auto insurance has become a necessity, and it is required in most states before we can register or operate a motor vehicle. But deciding on the right auto insurance coverage can be quite confusing. Before we order auto insurance we need to be certain that we understand our basic coverage, what is available for extra protection, what discounts and credits we may qualify for, and what minimum coverage may be required by law.

Our auto insurance basically provides financial protection

for damages resulting from our automobile for which we may be held legally liable. The basic coverage should include bodily injury and property damage insurance. Bodily injury protects us in the event we are legally liable for injury to another person as the result of an automobile accident. The first limit is the amount the policy will pay as a result of injury to any one person. The second limit is the maximum amount the policy will pay for injuries to more than one person. A coverage amount of $100,000/ $200,000 is usually adequate. Property damage insurance protects us against financial loss for damage to another's property, if we're legally liable for that damage. A coverage of $50,000 is usually recommended for property damage. These two coverages are the most important part of our auto policy since they protect us against our greatest potential financial losses.

Even if we receive medical benefits from another source, we may want to carry insurance coverage, which provides benefits— regardless of who's at fault in an auto accident—for ourselves as well as passengers in our vehicle. No-fault coverage is optional in some locations and mandatory in others. It typically pays for medical expenses, hospital costs, and rehabilitation costs up to the limit of the policy. It may also include compensation for loss of income to cover part of our salaries, essential household expenses, and accidental death benefits.

If our vehicles are financed, our banks or credit unions usually require that we carry coverage for damage to our autos. If our vehicles aren't financed, our decision to carry this coverage should be based on the vehicles' actual cash value and whether we could afford the out-of-pocket loss in the event of an accident.

There are two types of physical damage coverage:

- Damage other than collision (Comprehensive)—protects us against loss when our cars are damaged by something other than collision or upset. It pays us, minus the deductible and subject to our vehicles' depreciation, for damage to our vehicles caused by fire, theft, earthquake, flood, hail, windstorm, vandalism, and other perils not specifically excluded in the policy. Glass breakage is usually also covered.

- Collision—pays us, minus the deductible and subject to our vehicles' depreciation, for damage to our vehicles caused by collision or upset.

The insurance rates we pay for our cars can vary dramatically depending on the insurance company, agent, or broker we choose, the coverage we request and the kind of cars we drive. Listed below are some helpful tips for lowering auto insurance costs from the Insurance Information Institute, 110 William St., New York, NY 10038.

- Comparison shop. Prices for the same coverage can vary by hundreds of dollars, so it pays to shop around. Ask friends, check the Yellow Pages or call the state insurance department. Also check consumer guides, insurance agents or companies. This will give an idea of price ranges and tell which companies or agents have the lowest prices. But don't shop price alone.

  The insurer selected should offer both fair prices and excellent service. Quality personal service may cost a bit more, but provides added conveniences, so talk to a number of insurers to get a feeling for the quality of their service. Ask them about ways to lower costs. Check the financial ratings of the companies too. Then, when the field has been narrowed to three insurers, get price quotes.

- Ask for higher deductibles. Deductibles represent the amount of money a person pays before he makes a claim. By requesting higher deductibles on collision and comprehensive coverage, insurance costs can be lowered substantially. For example, increasing the deductible from $200 to $500 could reduce the collision cost by fifteen to thirty percent.

- Drop collision and/or comprehensive coverage on older cars. It may not be cost effective to have collision or comprehensive coverage on cars worth less than $1000 because any claim would not substantially exceed annual insurance costs and deductible amounts. Auto dealers, credit unions, and banks can provide information on the worth of a car.

- Eliminate duplicate medical coverage. If a person has adequate health insurance, he may be paying for duplicate medical coverage in his auto policy. In some states, eliminating this coverage could lower the personal injury protection (PIP) cost by up to forty percent.

- Buy a "low profile" car. Before buying a new or used car, check into insurance costs. Cars that are expensive to repair, or that are favorite targets for thieves, have much higher insurance costs. Write to the Insurance Institute for Highway Safety, 1005 North Glebe Road, Arlington, VA 22201 and ask for the Highway Loss Data Chart.

- Consider area insurance cost if making a move. Costs tend to be lowest in rural communities and highest in center cities where there is more traffic congestion.

- Take advantage of low-mileage discounts. Some companies offer discounts to motorists who drive fewer than a predetermined number of miles a year.

- Find out about automatic seat belt or air bag discounts. You may be able to take advantage of discounts on some coverage if you have automatic seat belts and/or air bags.

- Inquire about other discounts. Some insurers offer discounts for more than one car, no accidents in three years, drivers over fifty years of age, driver training courses, anti-theft devices, anti-lock brakes, and good grades for students.

CHAPTER ELEVEN

ACHIEVING GOOD CREDIT

Our need to maintain good credit is of paramount importance. We typically will not have the money ourselves to purchase many of the big ticket items in our lives, such as a car, house, or college education. Even our ability to obtain medication and medical treatment may very well depend on our credit ratings. Thus, having access to credit is very important if we are to acquire and enjoy most major assets during our lifetime. Furthermore, changes in our lives, such as divorce, loss of income, relocation, retirement, education for our children, and loss of a spouse, may all trigger a need for us to obtain credit or review our current credit history. Maintaining a good credit history and establishing sources of credit should always be a part of our financial planning.

Building a Credit History

Although lenders consider a variety of factors in deciding whether to give us credit, most of them rely heavily on our credit histories. So, building a good credit history is essential to us if we want to be able to borrow money. If we have no reported credit history, it may take time for us to establish credit.

If a person does not have a credit history, he should begin to build one. If he has a steady income and has lived in the same area for at least a year, he should try applying for credit with a local business, such as a department store. Or he might borrow a small amount from his credit union or the bank where he has checking and savings accounts. A local bank or department store may approve his credit application even if he does not meet the standards of larger creditors. Before he applies for credit, he should ask whether the creditor reports credit history information to credit bureaus serving his area. Most creditors do, but some do not. If possible, he should try to get credit that will be reported. This builds his credit history.

If a person does not have a credit file, he can visit or write his local credit bureau and request that a file be started on him. Most credit reporting agencies will require that he provide them with his identification, his address (last five years), Social Security number, place of employment and verification of income. If he has prior creditors, he should contact them to obtain copies of his last credit transactions. Also, if he has a bank account, he should attempt to get a letter of reference from his banker and submit these to the credit reporting agency.

A person should open checking and savings accounts at several financial institutions if he does not have any. These may be useful as credit references and as easier sources of credit because of his ongoing relationship. Most creditors will not extend credit unless a person has at least three good credit references. He should apply for a major credit card. If he does not qualify, he can check to see if he can offer collateral or have someone cosign.

The Federal Trade Commission enforces a number of federal credit laws and provides free brochures and publications on many credit-related issues. The Federal Reserve System and the Federal Deposit Insurance Corporation also provide free consumer pamphlets and handbooks on a variety of credit topics. Much of the following information was provided by these sources.

Conducting Your Own Credit Review

Even if we are not currently looking to borrow money, we should routinely check to find out what information is in our credit files. Some financial advisors suggest that consumers review their credit reports every three or four years to check for inaccuracies or omissions. This could be especially important if we are considering making a future major purchase, such as buying a home. Checking in advance on the accuracy of information in our credit files could speed the credit-granting process.

To find which credit bureaus have our file, we can check the Yellow Pages under credit bureaus or credit reporting agencies for the phone numbers and addresses of the bureaus near us. When contacting them, we will need to give all identifying information, such as full name, Social Security number, current address, former address, and spouse's name (if applicable). Ordinarily, a credit bureau will charge about ten dollars to thirty dollars to give us our credit file information. To get a complete credit picture, we ought to ask all local credit bureaus if they maintain files on us.

Credit reporting agencies, often called credit bureaus, are companies that gather information on credit users and sell that information in the form of credit reports to credit grantors, such as banks, finance companies, and retailers. Credit bureaus keep records of consumers' debts and how regularly these debts are repaid. They gather information from creditors who send computer tapes or other payment data to credit bureaus, usually on a monthly basis, showing what each account-holder owes or has paid. The data show if payments are up-to-date or overdue, and if any action has been taken to collect overdue bills. The credit bureau adds this data to existing information in consumer files, creating a month-by-month history of activity on consumer accounts.

If someone has been denied credit because of information that was supplied by a credit bureau, the Fair Credit Reporting Act requires the creditor to give him the name and address of the credit bureau that supplied the information. If he contacts that bureau to learn what is in his file within thirty days of receiving a denial notice, the information is free.

Once a person has received his credit report, he needs to

179

make sure that he understands the report. Often, credit reports are computer coded for recordkeeping purposes, and thus difficult to understand. If a person does not understand his report, the credit bureau is required by law to give him an explanation of what his report says. If he still does not understand, he can set up an appointment with a credit counselor to discuss his report.

Our credit files may not contain information on all of the accounts we have with creditors. Although most national department store and all-purpose bank credit card accounts will be included in our files, not all creditors supply information to credit bureaus. For example, some travel-and-entertainment and gasoline card companies, local retailers, and credit unions do not report to credit bureaus.

No one can legally do a credit check on us without our authorization. Each time that we complete a credit application, a credit report is usually run on us and reported to the credit bureau. Furthermore, sometimes credit checks are run on us without our knowledge, usually by places that offer instant credit, like used car lots and discount stores. If no credit account is opened as a result, then perspective creditors may view all the inquiries as rejections of our applications for credit and feel uneasy in extending us credit. If someone discovers that there are unauthorized or numerous inquiries on his report, he should write a letter to the credit bureau and request that these inquiries be removed.

If any of us has been told that we were denied credit because of an "insufficient credit file" or "no credit file" and we have accounts with creditors that do not appear in our credit files, we can ask the credit bureau to add this information to future reports. Although they are not required to do so, for a fee many credit bureaus will add other accounts, if verifiable, to our credit files.

Under the Fair Credit Reporting Act, credit bureaus can report most negative information for no more than seven years. The seven-year period runs from the date of the last regularly scheduled payment that was made before the account became delinquent unless the creditor later took action on the account—

such as charging if off or obtaining a judgment for the amount due. If a creditor took such an action, the seven years would run from the date of that event. For example, if a retailer turned over a past-due account to a collection agency in 1987, a credit bureau may report this event until 1994. However, if a payment was made after 1987 on this account, this action would not extend the permissible reporting period beyond 1994.

There are exceptions to the seven-year rule. Bankruptcies may be reported for ten years. Also, any negative credit-history information may be reported indefinitely in three circumstances:

* If applying for $50,000 or more in credit.
* If applying for a life insurance policy with a face amount of $50,000, or more.
* If applying for a job paying $20,000 or more (and the employer requests a credit report in connection with the application).

We can contact the credit bureau if we believe negative information is being reported beyond the permitted period and ask that it be removed.

Correcting Errors in Your Credit Report

Our credit file may contain errors that can affect our chances of obtaining credit in the future. Under the Fair Credit Reporting Act, we are entitled to have incomplete or inaccurate information corrected without charge.

If we dispute information in our reports, the credit bureau must reinvestigate it within a "reasonable period of time," unless it believes the dispute is "frivolous or irrelevant." To check on the accuracy of a disputed item, the credit bureau will ask the creditor in question what its records show. If the disputed item is on the public record, the credit bureau will check there instead. If a disputed item cannot be verified, the credit bureau must delete it. If an item contains erroneous information, the credit bureau must correct the error. If the item is incomplete, the bureau must complete it. For example, if our files showed accounts that belong to another person, the credit bureau would have to delete them. If it showed that we were late in making payments but failed to show that you are no longer delinquent, the credit bureau would have to add information to show that our payments are now current. Also, at our request, the credit bureau must send a notice of the correction to any creditor who has checked our files in the past six months.

If the reinvestigation does not resolve our disputes, the Fair Credit Reporting Act permits us to file a statement of up to one hundred words with the credit bureau explaining our side of the story.

Dealing with Poor Credit History

Before creditors will give us credit, they look to how we have paid our bills in the past. Negative information in our credit file may lead creditors to deny us credit. Information that is considered negative includes late payments, repossessions, accounts turned over to a collection agency, charge-offs (accounts viewed as a "loss" by a creditor), judgments, liens, and bankruptcy.

A poor credit history that is accurate cannot be changed. There is nothing that we (or anyone else) can do to require a credit bureau to remove accurate information from our credit reports until the reporting period has expired. However, this does not necessarily mean that we will be unable to obtain credit during the period. Because creditors set their own credit-granting standards, not all of them look at our credit history in the same way. Some creditors may look only at more recent years to evaluate us for credit, and they may grant us credit if our bill-paying history has improved. Before applying for credit, it may be useful to contact creditors informally to discuss their credit standards.

If we cannot obtain credit based on our own credit history, we may be able to do so if someone who has a good credit history cosigns a loan for us—this means the cosigner agrees to pay if we do not. Or we may be able to obtain a small loan or a credit card with a low dollar limit by using our savings accounts as collateral. If we pay promptly and our creditors report to a credit bureau, this new information will improve our credit history picture.

Coping with Mounting Bills

A sudden illness or the loss of our jobs may make it impossible for us to pay our bills on time. Whatever our situation, if we find that we cannot make our payments, we should contact our creditors at once. We should try to work out a modified payment plan with our creditors that reduces our payments to a more manageable level. If we have paid promptly in the past, they may be willing to work with us. Do not wait until the account is turned over to a debt collector. At that point, the creditor has given up on us. Most creditors do not want to spend time and money to collect delinquent accounts—all they want is their money! Therefore, in most cases, our creditors will be willing to work with us through our crises. For example, we may want to offer our creditors interest payments on our debts and delay payments on our principal until our condition changes; also, we ought to check to see if our debts are covered by a payment protection plan or other insurance that would pay our debts. In some cases we may be able to get our creditors to accept a partial payment as satisfaction in full for our debts. In any event, we should maintain an open dialogue with our creditors keeping them abreast of our situation.

If we do work out a debt-repayment plan, we should ask our creditors to report our new, smaller payments to the credit bureau as timely. Otherwise, the credit bureau may report these payments as delinquent because we are paying less than the amount agreed to in our original credit agreements.

Automobile loans may present special problems. Most automobile financing agreements permit our creditors to repossess our cars any time that we are in default on our payments. No advance notice is required. If our cars are repossessed, we may have to pay the full balance due on the loan, as well as towing and storage costs, to get them back. If we cannot do this, the creditor may sell the car. We should not wait until we are in default. Rather, we should try to solve the problem with our creditor when we realize we will not be able to meet our payments. It may be better to sell the cars ourself and pay off our debts. This would avoid the added costs of repossession and a negative entry on our credit reports.

Understanding the Cost of Credit

If we are thinking of borrowing or opening a credit account, our first step should be to figure out how much it will cost us and whether we can afford it. Then we should shop around for the best terms.

Two laws help us compare costs:
- Truth in Lending requires creditors to give us certain basic information about the cost of buying on credit or taking out a loan. These "disclosures" can help us shop around for the best deal.
- Consumer Leasing disclosures can help us compare the cost and terms of one lease with another and with the cost and terms of buying for cash or on credit.

Credit costs vary. By remembering two terms, we can compare credit prices from different sources. Under Truth in Lending, the creditor must tell us (in writing and before we sign any agreement) the finance charge and the annual percentage rate.

The finance charge is the total dollar amount we pay to use credit. It includes interest costs, and other costs, such as service charges and some credit-related insurance premiums.

CHAPTER TWELVE

PROTECTING YOUR PRIVACY

*T*he 1990s and the turn of the century will bring dramatic improvements in the ability to collect and disseminate personal, financial, and medical information on the general public. There is a growing concern over technology and its connection to the invasion of privacy in the workplace and at home. People are also concerned about the escalating problems of credit card, mail, and telephone fraud; unwanted mail and telemarketing calls; employer surveillance; and what they can do to keep from becoming victims.

There are many ways we can help to protect our privacy and personal records. When we are filling out an application for credit, insurance, or a job we should always ask how the information we give about ourselves will be used. Who has access to it? Will the information be exchanged with other companies? How long is the information kept? How often is it updated?

Protecting Credit Records

With credit bureaus collecting more and more information on consumers' credit habits, we need to check our credit records periodically, correct any inaccuracies, and be sure that there have been no improper releases of our credit records. The three major credit bureau companies (Equifax, Trans Union, and TRW) will agree not to release a person's name and other information for marketing purposes if he requests it.

We can contact these credit reporting companies for a copy of credit reports and other matters at the following addresses:

Equifax Credit Information Service
Wildwood Plaza
7200 Windy Hill
Suite 500
Marietta, GA 30067
800-685-1111

Trans Union Consumer Relations
25249 Country Club Blvd.
P.O. Box 7000
North Olmstead, OH 44070
216-779-7200

TRW Consumer Assistance Center
P.O. Box 749029
Dallas, TX 75374-9029
800-392-1122

Local credit bureaus are listed in the Yellow Pages under "Credit Reporting Agencies" or "Credit Bureaus."

Keep a list of credit card numbers, expiration dates, and the telephone number and address of each issuer in a safe place. When we use our credit cards, we should watch our card after giving it to a clerk. We should promptly take back the card after the clerk is finished with it and make sure that it is ours. We need to be certain that we tear up the carbons when we take our credit card receipts. Draw a line through any blank spaces above the total when signing credit card receipts, and never sign a blank receipt.

Sign new cards as soon as they arrive. Cut up and throw away expired cards. Save the purchase receipts until the credit card bill arrives. Then, promptly compare it with the receipts to check for possible unauthorized charges and billing errors.

We should write the card issuer promptly to report any questionable charges. Telephoning the card issuer to discuss the billing problem does not preserve our rights. Do not include written inquiries with payments. Instead, check the billing statement for the correct address for billing questions. The inquiry must be in writing and must be sent within sixty days to guarantee rights under the Fair Credit Billing Act.

If any credit cards are missing or stolen, report the loss as soon as possible to the card issuer. Check the credit card statement for a telephone number for reporting stolen credit cards. Follow up the phone calls with a letter to each card issuer. The letter should contain the card number, the date the card was missing, and the date the loss was reported.

If we report the loss before a credit card is used, the issuer cannot hold us responsible for any future unauthorized charges. If a thief uses our cards before we report them missing, the most we will owe for unauthorized charges is fifty dollars on each card. A special note of warning: If an automatic teller machine (ATM) card is lost or stolen, the consumer could lose as much as $500 if the card issuer is not notified within two business days after learning of the loss or theft.

We should not give our credit numbers over the telephone unless we initiated the call or already have accounts with the companies calling us. Never write credit card numbers on a post card or on the outside of an envelope.

We should not write our telephone numbers on credit or charge card purchase forms. Major credit and charge card providers generally do not require a telephone number for identification. However, where the merchant has no electronic or telephone connection with the card company to verify our accounts at the time of purchase, we may still be asked to provide a telephone number. If a merchant refuses to sell us goods or services because we will not provide personal information, such as our telephone numbers, we should report the store to the credit card company. The merchant might be violating his or her agreement with credit card companies. In the letter to the credit card company, the name and location of the merchant should be provided.

We should not permit a merchant to use our credit cards as a back-up in case our checks should bounce. Neither should we permit our credit or charge card account numbers to be written on our personal checks—particularly if the drivers' license number is being recorded as well.

Some states forbid merchants to record credit or charge card account numbers. Rather, they are permitted to only note whether we have a major credit or charge card as an indicator of our creditworthiness. Exceptions are services like "emergency check cashing," where we may have preapproved the use of our cards to guarantee our checks.

Note that the merchant might nevertheless refuse to accept our checks in some cases without credit card and telephone numbers. In such a case, we can decide to pay in cash or make our purchases from another merchant.

If we want to buy a product based on a telephone call from an unfamiliar company, we need to ask for the name, address and phone number where we can reach the caller after considering the offer. It is best to request and read written information before deciding to buy.

Keeping Your Medical and
Insurance Records Confidential

No one wants private information relating to medical treatment, hospitalization, and insurance coverage released without their permission. Every time we apply for individual life, health, or disability insurance, medical and other information about us is collected and, with our authorization, shared with a consortium of insurance companies. The Medical Information Bureau

(MIB) is a data bank used by over 700 insurance companies. MIB may have a brief coded report on applicants who have significant underwriting risks. The MIB uses this information to help insurers guard against fraud and high-risk coverage, such as AIDS and drug abuse.

We can obtain a free copy of our MIB files by writing or calling:

Medical Information Bureau
P.O. Box 105
Essex Station
Boston, MA 02112
Phone: (617) 426-3660

If the insurance company originating our files believes there is sensitive medical information recorded on our file, the company may require the MIB to send our medical files only to our doctors. In any event, we need to discuss our MIB file with our doctors periodically to make sure we understand what they say. We should ask our doctors to verify the accuracy and completeness.

Avoiding Mail and Telemarketing Frauds

Direct mail and telemarketing is used more and more by companies to reach consumers and by charitable organizations to reach potential contributors. This is an area which is ripe for fraud and invasion of privacy. If we do not want to receive unsolicited mail advertisements and telephone solicitations, we can usually write to the companies or organizations that are contacting us and ask to be removed from their mailing and telephone lists.

The Direct Marketing Association (DMA) operates the Mail Preference Service and Telephone Preference Service and provides telephone numbers and mailing information on consumers to subscribers. If a person wishes to have his name removed from the lists maintained by companies subscribing to these DMA services, he can write to:

Mail Preference Service
Direct Marketing Association
P.O. Box 9008
Farmingdale, NY 11735

or

Telephone Preference Service
Direct Marketing Association
P.O. Box 9015
Farmingdale, NY 11735

He will still get some mail and telephone calls, but this will significantly reduce the amount.

It is important that we try to control what information is kept about us. We should refuse to give more information to telemarketers than we feel is necessary or comfortable. We should ask for follow-up explanatory materials, and avoid giving any personal information unless we receive these materials. Some companies offer rebate, incentive, and warranty programs that benefit consumers. We should find out who has access to information we provide to participate in these programs. Some companies use this data to create mailing lists that are sold to marketers.

The U.S. Office of Consumer Affairs provides this information on avoiding mail fraud. More and more consumers are receiving misleading or downright fraudulent mail promotions. These promotions take several forms. Some examples are:

- Sweepstakes that require paying an entry fee or ordering a product
- Notices of prizes that require calling a 900 number or buying a product

- Mailings that look like they are from government agencies, but they are not
- Classified "employment" or "business opportunity" advertisements promising easy money for little work
- Prize awards that ask for credit card or bank account numbers

Consumers should be particularly suspicious of one of the most prevalent forms of mail fraud, notices that they have received a prize, in some cases, a very expensive prize like a car or vacation. Usually, they have to purchase a product, for example, a lifetime supply of cosmetics or large amount of vitamins, to be eligible to receive the prize. In fact, few of the prizes are awarded, and of those received, many are worthless.

The Alliance Against Fraud in Telemarketing, administered by the National Consumers League, has information about the dangers of these types of mail solicitations. We should contact our state or local consumer office or Better Business Bureau if we have any doubts about promotions we have received through the mail.

Safeguarding Your Privacy with Telecommunications

The telephone has become our primary form of communicating with each other, and is likely to be surpassed by the computer near the year 2000. The increasing use of voice mail, electronic mail, and cordless and cellular phones requires a critical look at how to protect our privacy and confidential information.

To protect our privacy on the telephone, we should keep in mind that cellular and cordless telephone conversations are easy to monitor. Never use these to conduct confidential conversations.

Some companies have taken steps to protect the privacy of voice and electronic mail. Typically a password is required to gain access to files. Several companies now make reading another person's electronic mail or listening to their voice mail a violation of corporate ethics and may result in disciplinary action.

Most of the time, however, there is a lack of adequate safeguards to protect the privacy of these messages.

Many companies may monitor voice and electronic mail to keep tabs on their employees. Therefore, it is best to consider voice and e-mail messages as non-private. We should never use these to discuss personal or other information which we would not want a third party to receive.

Telephone companies in a number of states offer a "caller ID" service. This service allows us to see the telephone number of the person calling us before we answer the telephone. If we do not recognize the incoming telephone number, or simply do not want to talk to the person, we can decide not to answer. If we are using caller ID service, we might consider using an answering machine or service so that we will not miss important calls from unfamiliar telephone numbers.

We may not want our telephones number revealed when we place a call to those who have caller ID. In such a case, we can check to see if our local telephone company offers a blocking system to prevent our telephone number from being displayed. Otherwise, we could place calls through an operator and request that our number not be revealed, or we could call from a pay phone.

Companies and organizations with 800 and 900 numbers might use a telephone number identification system to record our numbers when we call. They might also match our telephone numbers and addresses to add to customer lists for marketing purposes.

Protecting Yourself from Telephone Fraud

The Federal Trade Commission (FTC) provides these important facts for consumers on how we can protect ourselves from telephone fraud. The FTC estimates that fraudulent telemarketers swindle American consumers out of more than one billion dollars each year. They promote everything from useless water purifiers to interests in nonexistent oil wells.

The heart of the telemarketing operation is usually centered in a "boiler room," a rented office space filled with desks, telephones, and experienced salespeople. These people spend their days talking to hundreds of potential victims all across the country. Fraudulent telemarketers and sellers may reach us in several ways, but the telephone always plays an important role.

We may get a telephone call from a stranger who got our numbers from the telephone directory or a mailing list. A telemarketer calling from a boiler room may know, through a mailing list, our age, income, hobbies, marital status, and other information—all to help personalize the call. This is the classic telemarketing scam. We may make the telephone call ourselves in some cases, in response to a television, newspaper, magazine advertisement, or direct mail solicitation. However, just because we make the call does not mean the business is legitimate or that we should be any less cautious about buying or investing over the phone.

Automatic debit scams involve unauthorized debits (withdrawals) from our checking accounts. We may get a post card or a telephone call saying we have won a free prize or can qualify for a major credit card. If we respond to the offer, the caller may ask us to read off all of the numbers at the bottom of our checks. Sometimes we may not be told why this information is needed. Other times we may be told this account information will help ensure that we qualify for the offer. And, in some cases, the caller may explain this information will allow them to debit our account and ship the prize or process the fee for the credit card.

The telemarketer places our checking account information on a "demand draft," which is processed much like a check. However, unlike a check, the draft does not require our signatures. Our banks then pay the telemarketer's bank. And, we may not learn of the transaction until we receive our bank statements.

Automatic debit scams involve a fraud that is hard to detect, but there are some precautions we can take. We should never give our checking account number over the phone in response to solicitations from people we do not know. If anyone asks for our checking account numbers, we should ask them why they need this information. And, we should ask to review the company's offer in writing before we agree to a purchase.

Marketers of "gold" or "platinum" cards may promise in their ads that by participating in their credit programs, which might have an initiation fee of fifty dollars or more, we will be able to get major credit cards and improve our credit rating. But generally, this is not the case. Many of these credit card marketers—who often target people in lower-income areas through direct mail, television, or newspaper ads featuring "900" numbers—do not report to credit bureaus. And rarely can they help to secure lines of credit with other creditors. In fact, some of these cards only allow us to purchase merchandise from the marketer's own catalogue—and only after we have paid an extra charge.

Be skeptical of plans promising to secure major credit cards or erase bad credit. Contact the local consumer protection agency or the local Better Business Bureau (BBB) to learn if any complaints have been lodged against a particular marketer of "gold" or "platinum" cards. And be aware that unless marketers subscribe to credit bureaus, they are unable to report any information about a person's credit experience.

Telemarketing travel scams have many variations and often involve travel packages that sound legitimate. We may get a phone call or a postcard saying that we have been selected to receive a free trip. The card will tell us to call a toll-free or "900" number for details. On the phone, skilled salespeople will tell us, to be eligible for the free trip, we must join their travel club. Later, we may find another fee is required to make our reservations and we will have a telephone charge if we used the "900" line. In the end, we may never get our "free" trip because our reservations are never confirmed or we cannot comply with hard-to-meet or expensive conditions.

While it is sometimes difficult to tell a legitimate travel offer from a fraudulent one, there are some precautions we can take.

We should always be wary of "great deals," and before we pay for the trip, we should ask detailed questions that will give us clear answers. We should ask for the travel offer in writing, so we can check details. We can try to check the reliability of the travel company by calling our local consumer protection office or the local Better Business Bureau. But remember, they cannot vouch for the company, but only can tell us if they have any complaints logged under the company name.

Typical telephone investments sold by fraudulent telemarketers include coins, gemstones, interests in oil wells and gold mining operations, oil and gas leases, and the sale of precious metals such as gold and silver. Con artists direct their sales pitches to the universal desire to make money with little risk. A caller usually will say that we have been specially selected to participate in an unusual investment opportunity. The caller often requires that money, sometimes thousands of dollars, be transferred immediately because the "market is moving."

Be wary of telephone investment opportunities that are guaranteed to be risk-free and provide a high return. Before we give anyone our money, it is best to get written information about an investment, to invest in businesses we know something about, and to discuss the matter with a knowledgeable person.

If we have a complaint about a telemarketing sale, we should try to resolve complaints with the company first. If that does not work and we believe we have been defrauded, we can contact our local consumer protection agency or the Better Business Bureau to report the company.

If we believe we have been victims of a scam, we also can file a complaint with the FTC by writing to: Federal Trade Commission, Division of Marketing Practices, Washington, D.C. 20580. Although the FTC does not generally intervene in individual disputes, the information we provide may indicate a pattern of possible law violations requiring action by the Commission.

CONCLUSION

Knowing that immeasurable changes are occurring in the workplace, we can take the necessary steps to ensure that we find career success, financial prosperity, and a high quality of life. We can analyze tomorrow's job market, learn the right skills, and develop career plans to foster career self-reliance and fulfillment. We can manage our money, credit, insurance, and other resources for maximum benefit and enjoyment. We should be ready to develop the strategies that will bring success and satisfaction across a broad spectrum of important areas.

Personal happiness, wellness, and career satisfaction are significantly interdependent. Fulfillment in the nineties and beyond will require that we also focus on our health and fitness, our families, and our communities.

More and more stress will come from the highly competitive job market, increasing work demands, tougher personal relationships, family pressures, and other matters associated with high-tech living. We will need to find ways to balance all of these competing expectations, while at the same time meeting our own satisfaction and fulfillment.

Keep in mind that too much stress can lead to physical illness, such as high blood pressure, ulcers, and heart disease. It can also lead to depression, mental illness, and even suicide. Our recognition of the early signs of over-stress and doing something about them can make a big difference in the quality of our lives.

We will need to take charge of our health and fitness by getting proper nutrition, exercise and medical care. The best prescription for good health and wellness is following our own good judgment and our doctors' advice, and always keeping a positive attitude.

While getting our careers and personal development on track, we must also give special attention to promoting quality time at home with our families and loved ones.

Our lives should involve close, endearing relationships with family and friends. They should involve rewarding, satisfying careers and professional endeavors, as well as mentoring others by sharing our knowledge and experiences. The key to a happy and fulfilling personal and professional life is living to the fullest, always looking forward, planning ahead, valuing relationships, and taking good care of ourselves.

APPENDIX

Sources of State and Local Job Information

(Source: U.S. Department of Labor)

State and local job market and career information is available from state employment security agencies and State Occupational Information Coordinating Committees (SOICC's). State employment security agencies develop occupational projections and other job market information. SOICC's provide the title, address, and telephone number of state employment security agency directors of research and SOICC directors.

Alabama

Director, Labor Market Information, Alabama Department of Industrial Relations, 649 Monroe St., Room 422, Montgomery, AL 36130. Phone: (205) 242-8855

Director, Alabama Occupational Information Coordinating Committee, Bell Bldg., 207 Montgomery St., Suite 400, Montgomery, AL 36130. Phone: (205) 242-2990

Alaska

Chief, Research and Analysis, Alaska Department of Labor, P.O. Box 25501, Juneau, AK 99802-4500

Executive Director, Alaska Department of Labor, Research and Analysis Section, P.O. Box 25501, Juneau, AK 99802-5501. Phone: (907) 465-4518

American Samoa

Program Director, American Samoa State Occupational Information Coordinating Committee, Office of Manpower Resources, American Samoa Government, Pago Pago, AS 96799. Phone: (684) 633-4485

Arizona
Research Administrator, Arizona Department of Economic Security, 1789 West Jefferson, P.O. Box 6123, Site Code 733A, Phoenix, AZ 85005. Phone: (602) 542-3871

Executive Director, Arizona State Occupational Information Coordinating Committee, P.O. Box 6123, Site Code 897J, 1788 West Jefferson St., First Floor North, Phoenix, AZ 85005. Phone: (602) 542-3680

Arkansas
State and Labor Market Information, Arkansas Employment Security Division, P.O. Box 2981, Little Rock, AR 72203. Phone: (501) 682-1543

Executive Director, Arkansas Occupational Information Coordinating Committee, Arkansas Employment Security Division, Employment and Training Services, P.O. Box 2981, Little Rock, AR 72203. Phone: (501) 682-3159

California
Chief Employment Data and Research Division, California Employment Development Department, P.O. Box 942880, MIC 57, Sacramento, CA 94280-0001. Phone: (916) 427-4675

Executive Director, California Occupational Information Coordinating Committee, 800 Capitol Mall, MIC-67, Sacramento, CA 95814. Phone: (916) 323-6544

Colorado
Director, Labor Market Information, Chancey Building, 8th Floor, 1120 Lincoln St., Denver, CO 80203. Phone: (303) 894-2589

Director, Colorado Occupational Information Coordinating Committee, State Board Community College, 1391 Speer Blvd., Suite 600, Denver, CO 80204-2554. Phone: (303) 866-4488

Connecticut
Director, Research and Information, Employment Security Division, Connecticut Labor Department, 200 Folly Brook Blvd., Wethersfield, CT 06109. Phone: (203) 566-2120

Executive Director, Connecticut Occupational Information Coordinating Committee, Connecticut Department of Education, 25 Industrial Park Rd., Middletown, CT 06457. Phone: (203) 638-4042

Delaware
Chief, Office of Occupational and Labor Market Information, Delaware Department of Labor, University Plaza, Building D, P.O. Box 9029, Newark, DE 19702-9029. Phone: (302) 368-6962

Executive Director, Office of Occupational and Labor Market Information, Delaware Department of Labor, University Office Plaza, P.O. Box 9029, Newark, DE 19714-9029. Phone: (302) 368-6963

District of Columbia
Chief of Labor Market Information, District of Columbia Department of Employment Services, 500 C St. N.W., Room 201, Washington, DC 20001. Phone: (202) 639-1642

Executive Director, District of Columbia Occupational Information Coordinating Committee, Department of Employment Security Services, 500 C St. N.W., Room 215, Washington, DC 20001. Phone: (202) 639-1090.

Florida
Chief, Bureau of Labor Market Information, Florida Department of Labor and Employment Security, 2012 Capital Circle, S.E., Hartman Building, Tallahassee, FL 32399-0674. Phone: (904) 488-1048

Manager, Florida Department of Labor and Employment Security, Bureau of Labor Market Information, 2012 Capitol Circle, S.E., Hartman Bldg., Suite 200, Tallahassee, FL 32399-0673. Phone: (904) 488-7397

Georgia
Director, Labor Information System, Georgia Department of Labor, 223 Courtland St., NE., Atlanta, GA 30303. Phone: (404) 656-3177

Executive Director, Georgia Occupational Information Coordinating Committee, Department of Labor, 148 International Blvd., Sussex Place, Atlanta, GA 30303. Phone: (404) 656-9639

Guam
Executive Director, Guam State Occupational Information Coordinating Committee, Human Resource Development Agency, Jay Ease Bldg. Third Floor, P.O. Box 2817, Agana, GU 96910. Phone: (817) 646-9341

Hawaii
Chief, Research and Statistics Office, Hawaii Department of Labor and Industrial Relations, 830 Punchbowl St., Room 305, Honolulu, HI 96813. Phone: (808) 548-7639

Executive Director, Hawaii Occupational Information Coordinating Committee, 830 Punchbowl St., Room 315, Honolulu, HI 96813. Phone: (808) 548-3496

Idaho
Chief, Research and Analysis, Idaho Department of Employment, 317 Main St., Boise, ID 83735. Phone: (208) 334-6169

Director, Idaho Occupational Information Coordinating Committee, Len B. Jordan Bldg., Room 301, 650 West State St., Boise, ID 83720. Phone: (208) 334-3705

Illinois

Director, Economic Information and Analysis, Illinois Department of Employment Security, 401 South State St., 2 South, Chicago, IL 60605. Phone: (312) 793-2316
Executive Director, Illinois Occupational Information Coordinating Committee, 217 East Monroe, Suite 203, Springfield, IL 62706. Phone: (217) 785-0789

Indiana

Director, Labor Market Information, Indiana Department of Employment and Training Services, 10 North Senate Ave., Indianapolis, IN 46204. Phone: (317) 232-8456

Executive Director, Indiana Occupational Coordinating Committee, 309 West Washington St., Room 309, Indianapolis, IN 46204. Phone: (317) 232-8528

Iowa

Supervisor, Audit and Analysis Department, Iowa Department of Employment Services, 1000 East Grand Ave., Des Moines, IA 50319. Phone: (515) 281-8181

Executive Director, Iowa Occupational Information Coordinating Committee, Iowa Department of Economic Development, 200 East Grand Ave., Des Moines, IA 50309. Phone: (515) 242-4890

Kansas

Chief, Labor Market Information Services, Kansas Department of Human Resources, 401 Topeka Ave., Topeka, KS 66603. Phone: (913) 296-5058

Director, Kansas Occupational Information Coordinating Committee, 401 Topeka Ave., Topeka, KS 66603. Phone: (913) 296-1865

Kentucky

Manager, Labor Market Research and Analysis, Kentucky Department for Employment Services, 275 East Main St. - 1 East, Frankfort, KY 40621-0001. Phone: (502) 564-7976

Information Liaison/Manager, Kentucky Occupational Coordinating Committee, 275 East Main St. - 1 East, Frankfort, KY 40621-0001. Phone: (502) 564-4258

Louisiana

Director, Research and Statistics Division, Louisiana Department of Employment and Training, P.O. Box 94094, Baton Rouge, LA 70804-9094. Phone: (504) 342-3141

Coordinator, Louisiana Occupational Coordinating Committee, P.O. Box 94094, Baton Rouge, LA 70804-9094. Phone: (504) 342-5149

Maine

Director, Division of Economic Analysis and Research, Maine Department of Labor, Bureau of Employment Security, 20 Union St., Augusta, ME 04330. Phone: (207) 289-2271

Executive Director, Maine Occupational Information Coordinating Committee, State House Station 71, Augusta, ME 04333. Phone: (207) 289-2331

Maryland

Director, Office of Labor Market Analysis and Information, Maryland Department of Economic and Employment Development, 1100 North Eutaw St., Room 601, Baltimore, MD 21201. Phone: (301) 333-5000

Coordinator, Maryland Occupational Information Coordinating Committee, Department of Employment and Training, 1100 North Eutaw St., Room 600, Baltimore, MD 21201. Phone: (301) 333-5478

Massachusetts

Director of Research, Massachusetts Division of Employment Security, 19 Staniform St., 2nd Floor, Boston, MA 02114. Phone: (617) 727-6868

Director, Massachusetts Occupational Coordinating Committee, Massachusetts Division of Employment Security, Charles F. Hurley Bldg., 2nd Floor, Government Center, Boston, MA 02114. Phone: (617) 727-6718

Michigan

Director, Bureau of Research and Statistics, Michigan Employment Security Commission, 7310 Woodward Ave., Detroit, MI 48202. Phone: (313) 876-5445

Executive Coordinator, Michigan Occupational Information Coordinating Committee, Victor Office Center, Third Floor, 201 North Washington Square, Box 30015, Lansing, MI 48909. Phone: (517) 373-0363

Minnesota

Director, Research and Statistical Services, Minnesota Department of Jobs and Training, 390 North Robert St., 5th Floor, St. Paul, MN 55101. Phone: (612) 296-6546

Director, Minnesota Occupational Information Coordinating Committee, Minnesota Department of Economic Security, 690 American Center Bldg., 150 East Kellogg Blvd., St. Paul, MN 55101. Phone: (612) 296-2972

Mississippi

Chief, Labor Market Information Department, Mississippi Employment Security Commission, P.O. Box 1699, Jackson, MS 39215-1699. Phone: (601) 961-7424

Acting Executive Director, Department of Economic and Community Development, Labor Assistance Division, Mississippi Occupational Information Coordinating Committee Office, 301 West Pearl St., Jackson, MS 39203-3089. Phone: (601) 949-2002

Missouri

Chief, Research and Analysis, Missouri Division of Employment Security, P.O. Box 59, Jefferson City, MO 65104. Phone: (314) 751-3591

Director, Missouri Occupational Information Coordinating Committee, 421 East Dunklin St., Jefferson City, MO 65101. Phone: (314) 751-3800

Montana

Chief, Research and Analysis, Montana Department of Labor and Industry, P.O. Box 1728, Helena, MT 59624. Phone: (406) 444-2430

Program Manager, Montana Occupational Information Coordinating Committee, P.O. Box 1728, 1327 Lockey St., Second Floor, Helena, MT 58624. Phone: (406) 444-2741

Nebraska

Research Administrator, Labor Market Information, Nebraska Department of Labor, 550 South 16th St., P.O. Box 94600, Lincoln, NE 68509-4600. Phone: (402) 471-9964

Administrator, Nebraska Occupational Information Coordinating Committee, P.O. Box 94600, State House Station, Lincoln, NE 68509-4600. Phone: (402) 471-4845

Nevada

Chief, Employment Security Research, Nevada Employment Security Department, 500 East Third St., Carson City, NV 89713. Phone: (702) 687-4550

Executive Director, Nevada Occupational Information Coordinating Committee, 1923 North Carson St., Suite 211, Carson City, NV 89710. Phone: (702) 687-4577

New Hampshire

Director, Labor Market Information, New Hampshire Department of Employment Security, 32 South Main St., Concord, NH 03301-4587. Phone: (603) 228-4123

Director, New Hampshire State Occupational Information Coordinating Committee, 64B Old Suncook Rd., Concord, NH 03301. Phone: (603) 228-3349

New Jersey

Assistant Commissioner, Policy and Planning, New Jersey Department of Labor, John Fitch Plaza, Room 1010, Trenton, NJ 08625-0056. Phone: (609) 292-2643

Staff Director, New Jersey Occupational Information Coordinating Committee, 1008 Labor and Industry Bldg., CN 056, Trenton, NJ 08625-0056. Phone: (609) 292-2682

New Mexico

Chief, Economic Research and Analysis Bureau, New Mexico Department of Labor, 401 Broadway Boulevard, NE, P.O. Box 1928, Albuquerque, NM 87103. Phone: (505) 841-8645

Director, New Mexico Occupational Information Coordinating Committee, Tiwa Bldg., 401 Broadway NE., P.O. Box 1928, Albuquerque, NM 87103. Phone: (505) 841-8455

New York
Director, Division of Research and Statistics, New York State Department of Labor, State Campus, Bldg. 12, Room 400, Albany, NY 11240-0020. Phone: (518) 457-6181

Executive Director, New York Occupational Information Coordinating Committee, Department of Labor, Research and Statistics Division, State Campus, Bldg. 12, Room 400, Albany, NY 11240. Phone: (518) 457-6128

North Carolina
Director, Labor Market Information Division, North Carolina Employment Security Commission, P.O. 25903, Raleigh, NC 27611. Phone: (919) 733-2936

Executive Director, North Carolina Occupational Information Coordinating Committee, 1311 St. Mary's St., Suite 250, P.O. Box 27625, Raleigh, NC 27611. Phone: (919) 733-6700

North Dakota
Director, Research and Statistics, Job Service of North Dakota, P.O. Box 1537, Bismarck, ND 58502. Phone: (701) 224-2868

Coordinator, North Dakota Occupational Information Coordinating Committee, 1600 East Interstate, Suite 14, P.O. Box 1537, Bismarck, ND 58502-1537. Phone: (710) 224-2197

Ohio
Labor Market Information Division, Ohio Bureau of Employment Services, 145 South Front St., Columbus, OH 43215. Phone: (614) 644-2689

Director, Ohio Occupational Information Coordinating Committee, Division of LMI, Ohio Bureau of Employment Services, 1160 Dublin Rd., Bldg. A, Columbus, OH 43215. Phone: (614) 644-2689

Oklahoma
Director, Research Division, Oklahoma Employment Security Commission. 308 Will Rogers Memorial Ofc. Bldg., Oklahoma City, OK 73105. Phone: (405) 557-7116

Executive Director, Oklahoma Occupational Information Coordinating Committee, Department of Voc/Tech Education, 1500 W. 7th Ave., Stillwater, OK 74074. Phone: (405) 743-5198

Oregon
Assistant Administrator for Research and Statistics, Oregon Employment Division, 875 Union St., NE., Salem, OR 97311. Phone: (503) 378-3220

Executive Director, Oregon Occupational Coordinating Committee, 875 Union St., NE, Salem, OR 97311. Phone: (503) 378-8146

Pennsylvania
Director, Research and Statistics Division, Pennsylvania Department of Labor and Industry, 1216 Labor and Industry Building, Harrisburg, PA 17121. Phone: (717) 787-3265

Director, Pennsylvania Occupational Information Coordinating Committee, Pennsylvania Department of Labor and Industry, 1224 Labor and Industry Bldg., Harrisburg, PA 17120. Phone: (717) 787-8646

Puerto Rico
Director, Research and Statistics Division, Puerto Rico Department of Labor and Human Resources, 505 Munoz Rivera Ave., 20th Floor, Hato Rey, PR 00918. Phone: (809) 854-5385

Executive Director, Puerto Rico Occupational Information Coordinating Committee, 202 Del Cristo St., P.O. Box 6212, San Juan, PR 00936-6212. Phone: (809) 723-7110

Rhode Island
Administrator, Labor Market Information and Management Services, Rhode Island Department of Employment and Training, 101 Friendship St., Providence, RI 02903-3740. Phone: (401) 277-3730

Director, Rhode Island Occupational Information Coordinating Committee, 22 Hayes, St., Room 133, Providence, RI 02908. Phone: (401) 272-0830

South Carolina
Director, Labor Market Information, South Carolina Employment Security Commission, P.O. Box 995, Columbia, SC 29202. Phone: (803) 737-2660

Director, South Carolina Occupational Information Coordinating Committee, 1550 Gadsden St., P.O. Box 995, Columbia, SC 29202. Phone: (803) 737-2733

South Dakota
Director, Labor Information Center, South Dakota Department of Labor, P.O. Box 4730, Aberdeen, SD 57402-4730. Phone: (605) 622-2314

Director, South Dakota Occupational Information Coordinating Committee, South Dakota Department of Labor, 420 South Roosevelt St., P.O. Box 4730, Aberdeen, SD 57402-4730. Phone: (605) 622-2314

Tennessee
Director, Research and Statistics Division, Tennessee Department of Employment Security, 500 James Robertson Pkwy., 11th Floor, Nashville, TN 37245-1000. Phone: (615) 741-2284

Director, Tennessee Occupational Information Coordinating Committee, 500 James Robertson Pkwy., 11th Floor Volunteer Plaza, Nashville, TN 37219. Phone: (615) 741-6451

Texas
Director, Economic Research and Analysis, Texas Employment Commission, 15th and Congress Ave., Room 208T, Austin, TX 78778. Phone: (512) 463-2616

Director, Texas Occupational Information Coordinating Committee, Texas Employment Commission Building, Room 526T, 15th and Congress, Austin, TX 78778. Phone: (512) 463-2399

Utah
Director, Labor Market Information and Research, Utah Department of Employment Security, 140 East 300 South, P.O. Box 11249, Salt Lake City, UT 84147. Phone: (801) 536-7400

Executive Director, Utah Occupational Information Coordinating Committee. c/o Utah Department of Employment Security, P.O. Box 11249, 174 Social Hall Ave., Salt Lake City, UT 84147-0249. Phone: (801) 533-2274

Vermont
Director, Policy and Information, Vermont Department of Employment and Training, 5 Green Mountain Dr., P.O. Box 488, Montpelier, VT 05602. Phone: (802) 229-0311

Director, Vermont Occupational Information Coordinating Committee, Green Mountain Dr., P.O. Box 488, Montpelier, VT 05601-0488. Phone: (802) 229-0311

Virginia
Director, Economic Information Service Division, Virginia Employment Commission, P.O. Box 1358, Richmond, VA 23211. Phone: (804) 786-7496

Executive Director, Virginia Occupational Information Coordinating Committee, Virginia Employment Commission, 703 East Main St., P.O. Box 1358, Richmond, VA 23211. Phone: (804) 786-7496

Virgin Islands
Chief, Research and Analysis, Virgin Islands Department of Labor, P.O. Box 3159, St. Thomas, VI 00801. Phone: (809) 776-3700

Coordinator, Virgin Islands Occupational Information Coordinating Committee, P.O. Box 3359, St. Thomas, VI 00801. Phone: (809) 776-3700

Washington
Labor Market Information, Washington Employment Security Department, 212 Maple Park, Mail Stop KG-11, Olympia, WA 98504-5311. Phone: (206) 753-5114

Director, Washington Occupational Information Coordinating Committee, 212 Maple Park, MS KG-11, Olympia, WA 98504-5311. Phone: (206) 438-4803

West Virginia
Assistant Director, Labor and Economic Research, West Virginia Bureau of Employment Programs, 112 California Ave., Charleston, WV 25305-0112. Phone: (304) 348-2660

Executive Director, West Virginia Occupational Information Coordinating Committee, One Dunbar Plaza, Suite E, Dunbar, WV 25064. Phone: (304) 293-5314

Wisconsin
Director Labor Market Information Bureau, Wisconsin Department of Industry, Labor, and Human Relations, 201 East Washington Ave., Room 221, P.O. Box 7944, Madison, WI 53707. Phone: (608) 266-5843

Administrative Director, Wisconsin Occupational Information Coordinating Council, Division of Employment and Training Policy, 201 East Washington Ave., P.O. Box 7972, Madison, WI 53707. Phone: (608) 266-8012

Wyoming
Manager, Research and Planning, Division of Administration, Wyoming Department of Employment, P.O. Box 2760, Casper, WY 82602. Phone: (307) 235-3646

Executive Director, Wyoming Occupational Information Coordinating Council, P.O. Box 2760, 100 West Midwest, Casper, WY 82602. Phone: (307) 235-3642

National Office
United States Employment Service
200 Constitution Ave., N.W., Washington, DC 20210
Phone: (202) 529-0188

SELECTED
BIBLIOGRAPHY

Useful Books for Finding the Right Job

For Your Job Search:

Bolles, Richard N., *What Color Is Your Parachute?* Ten Speed Press, Box 7123, Berkeley, CA 94707. Updated annually.

Figler, Howard E., *The Complete Job Search Handbook: Presenting the Skills You Need to Get Any Job, And Have A Good Time Doing It.* Holt, Rinehart and Winston, 383 Madison Ave., New York, NY 10017. 1979.

Collard, Betsy A., *The High-Tech Career Book: Finding Your Place in Today's Job Market.* William Kaufmann, Inc., 95 1st St., Los Altos, CA 94022. 1986.

Durkin, Jon, *Mid-Life Career Changes.* Johnson O'Connor Research Foundation, Human Engineering Laboratory, 701 Sutter St., San Francisco, CA 94109.

Wegmann, Robert, Chapman, Robert, and Johnson, Miriam, *Work in the New Economy: Career and Job Seeking into the 21st Century.* JIST Works, 720 North Park Ave., Indianapolis, IN 46202. 1989.

Resumé Writing:

Parker, Yana, *The Damn Good Resumé Guide*. Ten Speed Press, Box 7123, Berkeley, CA 94707. 1986.

Interview Skills:

Hellman, Paul, *Ready, Aim, You're Hired: How to Job-Interview Successfully Anytime, Anywhere with Anyone*. AMACOM, 135 W. 50th St., New York, NY 10020. 1986.

Medley, H. Anthony, *Sweaty Palm—The Neglected Art of Being Interviewed*. Ten Speed Press, Box 7123, Berkeley, CA 94707. 1984.

Young Jobseekers:

Haldane, Bernard, Haldane, Jean, and Martin, Lowell, *Job Power: The Young People's Job Finding Guide*. Acropolis Books Ltd., 2400 17th St., NW, Washington, DC 20009. 1980.

Women Jobseekers:

I CAN Lists (Classifies homemaker skills under various job titles in business). Educational Testing Service, Publication Order Services, CN 6736, Princeton, NJ 08541-6736.

Disabled Workers:

Klein, Karen with Hope, Derrick, Carla, *Bouncing Back From Injury: How to Take Charge of Your Recuperation*. Prima Publishing & Communications, P.O. Box 1260BB, Rocklin, CA 95677. 1988.

Minority Applicants:

Johnson, Willis L., Ed., *Directory of Special Programs for Minority Group Members: Career Information Services, Employment Skills Banks, Financial Aid Sources*, 4th ed. Garrett Park Press, P.O. Box 190, Garrett Park, MD 20896. 1986.

Job Skill Requirements:

Occupational Outlook Handbook. Bureau of Labor Statistics, Superintendent of Documents, U.S. Government Printing Office, Washington, D.C. 20402. (Describes hundreds of occupations and thirty-five major industries.)

Guide for Occupational Exploration. Superintendent of Documents, U.S. Government Printing Office, Washington, D.C. 20402.

Training:
National Association of Trade and Technical Schools, 2251 Wisconsin Ave., N.W., Washington, D.C. 20009. Phone: (202) 333-1021. (A list of accredited technical schools.)

Federal Jobs:
U.S. Office of Personnel Management, Career America, Superintendent of Documents, U.S. Government Printing Office, Washington, D.C. 20402.

SAMPLE FUNCTIONAL RESUMÉ

Allison Springs
15 Hilton House
College de l'Art Libre
Smallville, CO 77717

(888) 736-3550

Job sought: Food Industry Sales Representative

Skills, education and experience

Negotiating skills: My participation in student government has developed my negotiating skills, enabling me both to persuade others of the advantages to them of a different position and to reach a compromise between people who wish to pursue different goals.

Promotional skills: The effective use of posters, displays, and other visual aids contributed greatly to my successful campaign for class office (Junior Class Vice President) committee projects, and fund raising efforts (which netted $15,000 for the junior class project).

Skills working with people: All the jobs I have had involve working closely with people on many different levels. As Vice President of the Junior Class, I balanced the concerns of different groups in order to reach a common goal. As a claims interviewer with a state public assistance agency, I dealt with people under very trying circumstances. As a research assistant with a law firm, I worked with both lawyers and clerical workers. And as a lifeguard (five summers), I learned how to manage groups. In addition, my work with the state and the law office has made me familiar with organizational procedures.

Chronology

September 1983 to present	Attended College de l'Art Libre in Smallville, Colorado. Will earn a Bachelor of Arts degree in political science. Elected Vice President of the Junior Class, managed successful fund drive, directed Harvest Celebration Committee, served on many other committees, and earned thirty-three percent of my college expenses.
January 1987 to present	Work as research assistant for the law office of McCall, McCrow, and McCow, 980 Main Street, Westrow, Colorado 77718. Supervisor: Jan Eagelli (666) 654-3211
September 1986 to December 1986	Served as claims interviewer intern for the Department of Public Assistance of the State of Colorado, 226 Park Street, Smallville, Colorado 77717. Supervisor: James Fish (666) 777-7717
1980–1985	Worked as lifeguard during the summer at the Shilo Pool, 46 Waterway, Shilo, Nebraska 77777.

References available on request.

SAMPLE CHRONOLOGICAL RESUMÉ

Allison Springs
15 Hilton House
College de l'Art Libre
Smallville, CO 77717

(888) 736-3550

Job sought: Food Industry Sales Representative

Education

September 1983 to June 1987	College de l'Art Libre College Lane Smallville, CO 77717	Vice President, Junior Class (raised $15,000 for junior project) Member College Service Club (2 years) Swim Team (4 years) Harvest Celebration Director Major: Political science with course in economics and accounting

Experience

Period employed January 1987 to present 10 hours per week	Employer McCall, McCrow, and Mc Cow 980 Main Street Westrow, Co 77718 Supervisor: Jan Eagelli	Job title and duties Research assistant: Conducted research on legal and other matters for members of the firm
September 1986 to December 1986 10 hours per week	Department of Public Assistance State of Colorado 226 Park Street Smallville, CO 77717 Supervisor: James Fish	Claims interviewer: Interviewed clients to determine their eligibility for various assistance programs Directed them to special administrators when appropriate
Summers 1980–1985	Shilo Pool 46 Waterway Shilo, NE 7777 Supervisor: Leander Neptune	Lifeguard: Insured safety of patrons by seeing that rules were obeyed, testing chemical content of the water, and inspecting mechanical equipment

References available on request.

Sample resumés from *Occupational Outlook Quarterly*.

INDEX

A

Abilities, *48–50*
Adaptability, *23, 67*
Adult education, *13, 99, 107*
Agencies
   – consumer, *191, 194*
   – labor and employment, *53, 199*
Annual interest rate, *184*
Annuities, *154*
Application (employment), *58*
Assets, *149*
Attaining Success, *8, 11, 17*
Automobile insurance, *173*

B

Banking, *150, 178*
Better Business Bureaus, *191*
Bonds, *153*
Budgeting, *142, 147*
Business organization, *89*
Business ownership, *77, 101*

C

Career
   – development, *19*
   – fulfillment, *17*
   – information, *52*
   – planning, *13, 19, 26*
   – stages, *20*
Cash flow, *147*
College (funding for), *142*
Communication, *117–123*
   – speaking, *120*
   – writing, *117*
Compensation, *45*
Computers, *105*
Consumer protection
   – credit cards, *186, 194*
   – financial institutions, *185-187*
   – telemarketing, *189, 194*
Corporation, *91*
Credit, *177–184*
   – building credit history, *177*
   – cost of credit, *184*
   – credit reporting agencies, *179, 186*
   – errors, *181*
   – records, *179, 185*
   – reports, *179, 185*

D

Death
- estate planning, *155–159*
- life insurance benefits, *161, 167*

Debt, *141*

Demotions, *71*

Developing career plans, *19*

Disability insurance, *170*

E

Earnings, *45*

Education, *13, 26, 48*

Employment
- information, *52*
- interviews, *59*
- occupational profiles, *28–45*
- transitions, *67–75*

Estate planning, *155–159*

Expenses, *148*

F

Financial institutions, *150*

Financial planning, *139–159*
- budgets, *142, 147*
- credit, *177*
- insurance, *161*
- investments, *152*
- taxes, *92, 97, 141, 157*
- trusts, *157*

401(k) Plans, *144*

Fraud
- credit cards, *186, 194*
- insurance, *172, 189*
- investments, *195*

Franchises, *86*

Fulfillment, *17*

G

Goals
- career, *19*

– financial, *140*

– insurance, *162, 167*

H

Health insurance, *170*

HMO, *172*

Home (obtaining funds to buy), *142*

I

Image, *63*

Information
- career and job information, *52*
- computer information, *108, 115*

Insurance, *161–176*
- auto, *173*
- health, *170*
- life, *161*

Internet, *55*

Interviews, *59*

Investments, *152*

J

Job
- earnings, *45*
- interviews, *59*
- orientation, *69*
- outlook, *26*
- skills, *48*
- transitions, *67–75*

K

Keeping a good image, *63*

L

Laws (affecting business ownership), *97*

Layoffs, *73*

Leadership, *49*

Life cycles, *20*

Life insurance, *162*

M

Mail fraud, *189*
Marketing talents, *52*
Medical insurance, *170*
Medical records, *188*
Money management, *139–159*
Moves (on the job), *70*

N

Negotiation, *125–136*
Net worth, *149*
Networking, *20, 98*

O

Occupational profiles, *28–45*
Organization (business forms of), *89*
Orientation, *69*

P

Participating, *61*
Partnership, *90*
Planning
  – career, *13, 19, 26*
  – estate, *155–159*
  – financial, *139–159*
  – investment, *152*
Preparing for unemployment, *73*
Presentations, *120*
Privacy, *185–195*
Promotions, *71*
Proprietorship, *89*

R

Recordkeeping, *8, 93*
Relocations, *72*
Reports
  – credit, *179, 185*
  – medical, *188*
Resumés, *55, 213*
Retirement income, *144*

S

Salaries, *45*
Skills, *48*
Software (computer), *110, 112*
Speaking, *120*
Starting a business, 77
Stocks, *154*
Stress, *197*
Subchapter S corporations, *92*

T

Taxes
  – corporate, *92*
  – estate, *156*
Telecommunication, *191*
Telemarketing, *189, 193*
Terminations, *73*
Training, *13, 48*
Transitions, *67–75*
Trusts, *157*

U

US savings bonds, *153*
US Treasury securities, *152*

W

Wellness, *7, 197*
Work (*see* "Job" and "Employment")
Writing, *117*